The
PALMISTRY
Workbook

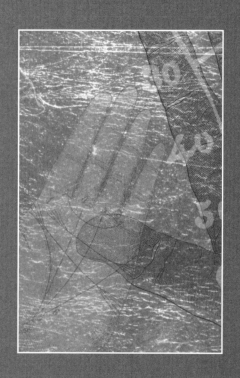

The PALMISTRY Workbook

A Step-by-Step Guide to the Art of Palm Reading

LAETICIA VALVERDE

METRO BOOKS
NEW YORK

This 2008 edition published by Metro Books,
by arrangement with Landsdowne Publishing Pty Ltd.

Text: Laeticia Valverde
Designer: Robyn Latimer
Illustrator: Corrie Cunningham
Additional illustrations: Penny Lovelock

Metro Books
122 Fifth Avenue
New York, NY 10011

ISBN-13: 978-1-4351-0817-2

Printed and bound in China.

1 3 5 7 9 10 8 6 4 2

The answers are before my eyes,
all is written in the palm.

CONTENTS

INTRODUCTION

WHAT IS PALMISTRY?

Palmistry is the ancient science of reading people's hands in order to gain insight into their lives. This practice is most closely associated with the gypsies, but though this link is a romantic one—supported by the presence of "gypsy" palm readers and fortune-tellers at many fairs—it is not necessarily the most accurate. In this book, you will learn of the palm-reading practices of many cultures of the past.

Indeed, palm reading has had its devotees in virtually every culture and era, and remains popular today. Perhaps one of the reasons for the fascination with palmistry is that, unlike other forms of divination, you can see the evidence before your eyes. While the skeptic could argue with the crystal ball or claim that the placement of Tarot cards is a coincidence, it is difficult to dispute facts that are etched into the palm.

The lines on our palms tell a wonderful story. Formed in utero at around seventeen weeks, these markings reveal much about our lives. We can also tell a great deal about the personality just by assessing the hand shape and the mounts that make up a hand. It is even possible to use palmistry to judge the ideal career for an individual.

Most people's knowledge of palmistry is limited to the lines and usually revolves around the mistaken belief that you can judge the length of a person's life by the length of the life line. While it is true that reading palms can give you some indications about a person's state of health, no palmist, however experienced, can accurately predict the year of death. As a beginning palm reader, use this book for the positive messages it can allow you to give people, rather than messages of doom.

THE POWER TO EFFECT CHANGE

Tell your subjects about the most favorable aspect of palmistry: that the owner of the palm is the only person who has the power to effect change in her own life. While others may be able to influence the direction we take, ultimately it is our own decisions that create the life we live. The markings on our palms are not static. They change along with changes to our lives and our personas. So it is important to realize that, should there be some indication in our palms that displeases us, it is well within our powers to change it.

When you do a reading for another person, point out the positives that you see in the palm and the ways they can counter any negative aspects that you may uncover. This is your purpose as a palmist—to help the subject see the good that is due to unfold in her life.

What can we read in a palm? Almost anything. The markings on our palms, our nails, our hand shapes, the size and shape of our fingers and knuckles, and the color of our skin and fingernails all contribute information about us. If you want to know about your love life, world travel, your future career, or your health, you will find many of the answers in your hand. Every line, every marking, and every part of your hand contains the pieces to the puzzle that is your life.

ABOUT THIS BOOK

Palmistry is a fascinating art and one in which, with practice, virtually everyone can excel. However, it is often difficult to get enough experience in order to gain competence. The purpose of this book is to give you the practice you need. It explains all aspects of the palm and the rest of the hand in a simple and logical manner, and provides tasks and exercises that will reinforce what you have learned. You can do the exercises at the end of a chapter many times; when you have been working on palmistry for some months, go back to the exercises and compare your answers at different times. You will be surprised at how much you have learned.

Keep a palmistry journal. Record your responses to all of the exercises here. Return to the journal often to look at the various features of your palm, and compare your readings as you increase your skills.

Each chapter ends with a review of the important facts it contains to support your learning and build your skills. When you first start out with palmistry, you will find yourself constantly referring back to your reference texts to check and double-check your facts. Use the reviews for this purpose. And note that having to check the facts is a vital part of learning a skill such as palmistry. It is important to feel comfortable with your skills in one area before moving on to the next. Give yourself time to develop your skills and try to avoid getting frustrated at not being able to remember the meanings of all the markings and lines from the outset. Use the many illustrations in this book and the reference images on pages 190–192, which contain a summary of the markings on the palms, when you need to refresh your memory.

Also, you will probably find that after a little practice it is your instinct that provides the answers. If you are unsure about the meaning of any features of the palm, close your eyes, hold the subject's hand in yours, and try to allow the answer to flow into your head. Most of the time it will; if it does not, however, do not worry. There will be another line or marking that will give you the answers you seek.

BEGINNING PALMISTRY

Refer constantly to your own hand as you read this book and others on the subject, and as you work through the exercises. This will help you to identify the many markings on the palm. Once you have identified something on your own hand, it will be easier to find it on someone else's. You will notice that the same line on one hand can look remarkably different on another. The fate line, for example, can appear in the most unusual places on some hands and in a variety of formations.

The best thing about starting palmistry is that you are bound to have a variety of eager subjects offering their palms for you to read. Also, your curious friends and relatives will not expect you to know everything—even a few items of interesting information will be enough to sate their curiosity temporarily. However, be sure to inform the people whose hands you are reading that you are still studying the subject and your answers cannot be seen as any more than an indication. Even when you are an experienced palm reader, you should give your subjects the same reassurance. Remind them that we are all individuals and that every hand contains subtle differences from any others you have read before.

It is important to realize that the knowledge that this book imparts is cumulative. You will be able to do simple readings based on your knowledge gained from the first few chapters, but you should always point out to your subjects the limitations of your readings. Be careful not to make bold pronouncements on character or events, but if you can come up with a positive statement, feel free to share it with your subject. Statements such as "You are very creative," or "You have so much dedication," or even "You have luck written all over your palm" are the kind of nonthreatening generalizations anyone would be glad to hear.

Enjoy learning the art of palm reading. If you take a methodical approach to your study and make a practice of observing other people's hands wherever you go, you will find that you will soon become absorbed in this fascinating practice.

CHAPTER ONE

THE HISTORY OF PALMISTRY

*Exploring the art and science of palmistry. How did palmistry originate?
How has it developed over thousands of years?*

Hands have long been a source of fascination to humans, so it is not surprising to learn that the ancient art of palmistry has been practiced for many thousands of years. Throughout history, this complex science has continued to intrigue people of virtually every culture and every level of society.

Palmistry is thought to have originated in China and India in around 2000 B.C., and continues to play a valued role in these cultures. The ancient Indian Vedic text, *The Laws of Manu*, dated 2000 B.C., contains the earliest known written reference to palmistry. The art of reading hands was also popular with the peoples of ancient civilizations, such as the Babylonians, Chaldeans, Egyptians, Greeks, Hebrews, Romans, and Tibetans.

THE INFLUENCE OF BUDDHISM

Buddhism, with its emphasis on a person's ability to create his own destiny, has a long tradition of the study of palmistry. For hundreds of years, Buddhist monks have studied the mysteries of the hands and passed down this knowledge to fellow practitioners within the monasteries. The study of palmistry, enriched with the Buddhist philosophy of life and combined with a spiritual understanding of humankind, has led to a deeply perceptive method of analysis.

Buddhists believe that we need to understand the psychological, philosophical, and spiritual growth of a person, and this view has helped expand palmistry into the holistic method of divination it is today. Rather than merely looking at the signs evident on a person's hand, palmists believe it necessary to ascertain that person's character first. This is why it is important, when reading a palm, to refer continually to other features and not just to examine one feature at a time, out of context, as the explanation that would arise from this feature in isolation may present a misleading overall picture.

FROM ARISTOTLE TO A GYPSY ART

The *Chiromantiae* by Aristotle (384–322 B.C.) is one of the earliest surviving texts on scientific hand analysis. The philosopher was particularly interested in the role that our hands play in determining our future and he wrote several texts on the subject. One of these texts was a reading for Alexander the Great, in which many predictions were made about his future.

After Aristotle, there was little focus on palmistry until the Greek physician Hippocrates (c. 460–377 B.C.) used the fingernails to aid diagnosis. Julius Caesar (100–44 B.C.) was also a devotee of palmistry, and much like some modern employers who use psychological testing to assess potential employees, he relied on the ancient art of palmistry to give him an insight into the nature of his men. Another Greek physician, Galen (c. 129–199 A.D.), brought palmistry back into the public arena.

Palmistry was branded "devil worship" by the Catholic Church and was forced underground for a number of years, with only the bravest of souls daring to express their interest in the matter. Gypsies asked their subjects to cross their palms with silver (the devil apparently feared the color silver and, naturally, the cross), but this only served to strengthen the perceived link between the devil and this esoteric art.

In the fifteenth and sixteenth centuries, palmistry was reintroduced to respectable society by the orator Paracelsus (1493–1541) and Robert Fludd (1574–1637). Palmistry spread throughout Europe in the sixteenth and seventeenth centuries, but during much of this period it was still considered the work of the devil. The church took a particularly grim view of fortune-tellers and persecuted those practicing the art. Palmistry was essentially a gypsy art at the time. As many gypsies had criminal reputations (deserved or not), a law was passed in England condemning to death any gypsy found breaking the law, and illegal actions included the reading of palms. Not surprisingly, it took a long time for palmistry to be accepted as a valid and informative practice.

A RESPECTABLE FORM OF DIVINATION

By the mid-seventeenth century, palmistry had shed its sinister undertones and came to be considered as a respectable form of divination, thanks to the publication of a translation of Aristotle's *Chiromantiae* by internationally renowned palmist Joannes Rothmann. This set off a spate of published works on the subject, including *Physiognomie and Chiromancie, Metoscopie* by Richard Saunders, famous for his numerous publications. The practice gained increasing prominence in the nineteenth century when Dr. Carl Carus, personal physician to the king of Saxony, used palm types to identify specific personalities.

Despite this, it was not until the twentieth century that palmistry started to become a true force with the arrival on the scene of a very gifted palmist, Cheiro, otherwise known as Count Louis Hamon. Cheiro was a gifted seer, a numerologist, and a talented astrologer, a combination that also rendered him a very accurate palmist. To add to his success, he had a talent for self-promotion.

Astrology has been popular since the Middle Ages, so it is no surprise that its popularity has permeated palmistry. Parts of the hands (the mounts and the fingers) have been named after seven well-known planets, which, in turn, were named after Roman and Greek gods and goddesses. For example, Venus was the goddess of love, and her attributes were subsequently passed on to the planet Venus, so it is no wonder that the large, fleshy mound below the thumb—whose presence indicates passion—should be named the mount of Venus. To gain an even greater understanding of the importance of the mounts and the fingers, many palmists immerse themselves in the study of astrology because the traits ascribed to the planets are manifest in these parts of the hand.

The greatest developments in palmistry and hand analysis have been achieved in the past hundred years. Police departments and hospitals now make use of palmistry, in particular through the study of dermatoglyphics (the study of the skin patterns on the surface of the fingers and palms). In 1901 Scotland Yard introduced fingerprinting as a method of identifying criminals, and since that time the scientific method of hand reading has become an intriguing method used to gain an understanding of the criminal mind. Undoubtedly, the greatest achievement of palmistry has been its ability to adapt to a changing society while remaining as relevant and intriguing as it was 4,000 years ago.

WORKBOOK EXERCISES

Understanding the history of palmistry will help you to become a truly intuitive palm reader. When you delve deeper in your research, you will discover that palmistry is not a static method, but one that is constantly evolving over time as more readers impart their own personality into their readings and methods.

1. Look through some other books on the history of palmistry (see Further Reading, page 180), and see what areas engage your interest. You will discover variations that appeal to you more than others, which makes it a good idea to try and discover all you can about palmistry so that you can really make it your own.

2. As you get further into this book, you will find that astrology and the ancient Greek and Roman gods and goddesses figure strongly in various aspects of the palm. Take a look through some literature on these topics. Write down the answers to the following questions in your journal.
   • What star sign are you?
   • What is your star sign's ruling planet?
   • Does your ruling planet have a god or goddess associated with it? If so, write down their name and five attributes commonly associated with them. Do these attributes resonate with you? Why or why not?

3. In your journal, write down your impressions of the development of palmistry over the years and where you think it might go in the future.

4. What role do you think palmistry will play in your life? Will you use your skills mainly for personal readings, for friends and family, or would you like to develop your skills and become a professional palmist? What image comes to mind when you think of a palmist?

CHAPTER TWO

THE HAND

Learn how to prepare for a palm reading; identify features of the hand and the hand types.

PREPARING FOR PALM READING

Most people associate palm reading with divining a person's future from the lines on the palms. While these lines are certainly an important aspect of palmistry, as this book will show you, it is vital to begin the study of the palm with the study of the hand itself. In this chapter, you will get some idea of the wealth of information that can be gained by the assessment of the hands alone.

HAND TYPES

As you begin this study, you may believe that most hands are quite similar. With practice, however, it is quite easy to differentiate the various types of hands by following a few basic steps. These steps are outlined within this chapter.

The best place to start looking is your own hand. Once you have decided what shape your own hand is, you will probably observe that many of the attributes ascribed to this shape match your own nature. Also, look at the hands of people around you and try to categorize them. This makes for fascinating practice.

Some palmists have identified up to eight hand types, with the foundations laid by Captain Stanislaus d'Arpentigny, who identified seven hand types in 1843. However, the elemental, philosophic, and nervous hands are now discounted by the majority of palmists as having little relevance in today's society. Rather, the attributes of these hand types, such as the bulging knuckles of the philosophic hand or the crisscrossed palm of the nervous hand, are considered as merely one aspect of the hand to be examined when doing a reading.

The vast majority of hands fit into five broad types: **square***, **conic**, **spatulate**, **psychic**, and the **mixed hand**. These shapes are discussed in detail on pages 24–35.

HAND COLOR

The coloring of the hand is also important. It can provide you with valuable information about the person's health and well-being:

- Pale skin with a bluish tinge can be a sign of weakness or a sickly disposition.
- Pink signals good health.
- Red can be a sign of passion and a fiery nature, or of aggression or stress.
- Yellow can show digestive problems.
- Gray indicates circulation problems.

You will need to use your judgment when assessing color, particularly as this is not a characteristic that is assessable on all hands. For people with darker skin, it is often difficult to judge the color of the skin on the palm. If this is the case, then just move on to examining another aspect of the hand. You are bound to find something of interest in another area.

FLEXIBILITY

Flexibility is another criterion we can use to assess a hand. The amount of movement it is capable of can reveal much about its owner. When reading a palm, the way to test its flexibility is by bending it gently forward and backward and rotating it clockwise and counterclockwise. People with moderately flexible hands and fingers tend to be quite adaptable and will happily listen to another's point of view before forming their own opinion. However, the opposite can be said of those with stiff, rigid hands—presuming that the rigidity is not due to an injury or an illness such as arthritis, in which case it should be ignored. People with naturally rigid hands tend to be stubborn and very opinionated— almost nothing will make them change their minds. People with hands that are extremely flexible, however, may bend so readily to another's will that they allow themselves to be taken advantage of and need to learn to trust in themselves.

*Terms described in the glossary (pages 180–185) are highlighted in **bold** the first time they are used.*

SKIN TEXTURE

Texture is also important and tends to be closely associated with the hand types. For example, the skin on square hands tends to be coarser than the skin on psychic hands. In general, people with a coarse skin texture tend to be a little insensitive in their affairs with others, as they do not always consider the impact of their behavior on others. Fine skin texture is indicative of a sensitive soul, a creative person with an innate love of beauty. People with medium-texture skins are generally outgoing in attitude and have a calm approach to life. However, you will not always be able to determine what the subject's natural skin texture is. Remember that you will need to take into account the effects of aging, years of work in the sun, and the damage inflicted by years of washing the dishes without gloves or doing other forms of manual labor without gloves for protection.

HAND SHAPE AND GENETICS

You will note that many people share the hand shapes and lines on the palm with their parents. However, as a child grows, the hand used most frequently—the **active hand**—may begin to take on an entirely new shape. Eczema and vitiligo also play a role in the appearance of the skin, but again must not be taken into consideration when doing a reading, particularly if the condition is transitory in nature.

INFLUENCES ON HAND SHAPE

When examining someone's hands, it is vital to ask whether that person suffers from any conditions of the joints or muscles, as this can substantially alter the appearance of the hands. For example, arthritis causes knotty fingers that are typically associated with the philosopher's hand (the hand of an analytical thinker), but the philosophical traits will be present only if other signs point to such a trait. You will therefore need to find out what the appearance of the hand was like before the condition appeared and base your reading on this—or you will have to ignore this aspect of the reading completely.

CATEGORIZING HAND TYPES

The five basic hand types discussed in this chapter—square, conic, spatulate, psychic, and the mixed hand—are the kinds of hands you are likely to encounter when reading palms. An alternative method, categorizing hands by the elements of Earth, Fire, Air, and Water, is relatively recent. This is a classification based on the modern form of scientific hand reading rather than traditional palmistry, which is what this book is about. Scientific, or diagnostic, hand reading is very similar in its basis to palmistry, the main difference being that many palmists use their intuition or psychic powers to some degree when undertaking a reading, while hand readers do not—theirs is a purely scientific study.

While traditional palmistry has been around for thousands of years, the scientific manner of hand analysis is relatively recent. One of the most obvious differences between traditional palmistry and scientific hand analysis is in the manner of hand classification. While palmistry distinguishes up to seven or eight hand types, scientific hand reading as noted above contains four, based on the elements. Dr. Carl Carus, mentioned in the last chapter, formulated a new system of hand shape classification in 1846. He divided hands into four types: motoric, elementary, sensitive, and psychic. His descriptions of these hand types fitted neatly with the typology of the four elements. The **Fire hand** has a long palm with short fingers, the **Earth hand** has a square palm with short fingers, the **Air hand** has a square palm with long fingers, and the **Water hand** has a rectangular hand with long fingers.

IDENTIFYING HAND SHAPES

To help identify a hand shape, you may wish to make a handprint or a photocopy of a person's hands. Seeing the shape in black and white will make it easier for you to assess the shape than will looking at a three-dimensional hand in living color. See pages 22–23 for an explanation of the print-making process.

Also, keep looking at people's hands to develop your powers of observation and to help identify their shapes. You will probably notice that people who work outdoors often have square or spatulate hands, while a large number of celebrities, particularly those involved in acting and music, have the attractive conic hands common to creative types.

MAKING PRINTS

As you begin to learn about palmistry, you will find it useful to make prints of the hands of relatives and friends. You can use these to check for lines and markings as you learn about them. It is also a good idea to make copies of the palms you read as you work your way through this book. Refer to these prints again later in your studies to see if you come up with any new insights. You should also make copies of your own palm, and those of family members, about every five years, and note the differences that develop.

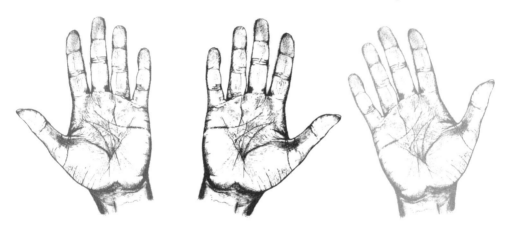

There are two good methods for making prints from palms. The first is to obtain a good-quality black-and-white or color photocopy, and the second is to take an ink imprint. To make an ink imprint, you will need the following:
- tube of black water-based block printing ink from an art supply store
- rubber roller, approximately 4 inches wide
- good-quality white paper
- sheet of glass, linoleum, or newspaper for applying the ink
- thin pad of foam to provide a cushion for the paper

Place the foam on a firm work surface and then place the paper over the top. Spread the ink on the newspaper, linoleum, or glass sheeting and then smooth the roller over this surface to obtain an equal coverage of ink. Now thoroughly cover the surface of your subject's palm.

Ask your subject to place the palm firmly on the paper in a comfortable manner so the spread of the fingers is as natural as possible. Get your subject to show you how the fingers fall naturally before you do so, and make notes if there are any marked differences in the splay of the fingers when the hand is pressed down onto paper. Apply pressure to the whole hand, paying extra attention to the center of the palm and the area of the mounts. Remove the hand from the paper and allow the print to dry.

You should also make notes for any attributes that cannot be recorded in a handprint, such as the color of the skin, the amount of flexibility, the subject's age, and any other details you consider relevant.

WORKBOOK EXERCISES

Using the steps listed above, make handprints of five subjects and compare the prints to the subjects' hands. Take note of the following:

1. Do some lines or features stand out more on the prints or the hands?
2. Can you notice features on the prints that you didn't note on the subject's hands?
3. Note any features that haven't come out in the print process; for example, the color of the skin, shape of the fingernails, or any other features you deem relevant.
4. Make a note of the date the print was taken and file it away so that you can make a print in a year's time and see whether the subject's hands have altered.

THE SQUARE HAND

To identify a square hand, it often helps to start by looking at the palm. A square hand will feature a palm that is as long as it is wide and is undeniably squared-off in appearance, with no rounded edges or features. The fingers on this hand are also square in appearance, with the top of the fingertips appearing flat rather than rounded.

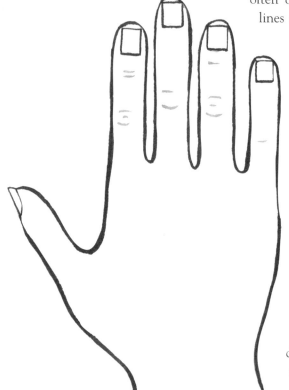

The lines on a square hand are usually simple and often only feature the four primary, or basic, lines on the palm (the **head, heart, life,** and **fate lines**—see Chapter Three), and rarely many secondary lines. The lines on a square palm tend to be deep, straight, and short rather than long and curved.

People with square hands are usually blessed with dexterity. Often, they are gardeners, carpenters, or successful businesspeople, particularly those who have worked their way to the top. People with square hands will enjoy the opportunity of spending their time away from work in the great outdoors.

People with square hands tend to be meticulous. They love to organize and plan everything down to the tiniest detail, and may become upset if anything untoward affects their well-ordered lives. These people are usually realists, enjoy physical activity, and are very good with money—they actually enjoy saving. They are practical and sensible and do not like to deviate from their routine.

Pay particular attention to the thumb when reading a square palm. If it is rigid, then the owner will tend to be even less adaptable to circumstances than those with square hands and flexible thumbs.

The fingers on a square hand can be short, medium, or long in relation to the palm, and may be smooth or **knotted**. A square hand with long, squared-off fingers shows a person who is highly likely to succeed in their chosen career. A square palm featuring short fingers shows a person who is inclined to follow the lead of others rather than striking out for success alone.

Reading a square hand is quite a challenge, as people with square hands often tend to be skeptics and therefore not inclined to believe in esoteric arts such as palmistry. However, just like everyone else, square-handed people will happily listen to a litany of their good points.

 WORKBOOK EXERCISES FOR THE SQUARE–HANDED

1. To help boost positive qualities and diminish negative qualities, square-handed individuals should spend a few minutes per day reflecting on the following:
   • I am a unique individual.
   • My creativity is bursting to come to the fore.
   • I accept everything that life brings my way.
2. List five personal qualities that you feel enrich your life.
3. List five qualities you'd like to nurture in yourself.
4. Compose a ten-point plan of how you can use your strengths to help turn your weaknesses into positive attributes. What are three concrete steps that you can take today? How can you incorporate these steps into your everyday life?

THE CONIC HAND

Conic hands are instantly identifiable—they are beautiful hands. Hands of this type taper slightly at the tips of the fingers or the base of the palm, and also tend to be slender, with fine skin texture. People with conic hands are impulsive; it is most often the conic-handed person who will marry a person she has known only for a single day.

People with conic hands are firm believers in the importance of first impressions. They are sentimental and very romantic. Reason plays little role in their decisions. They love people and they also need variety in their lives. They may therefore have different groups of friends to cater to their different interests: work friends, sport friends, movie friends, and so on.

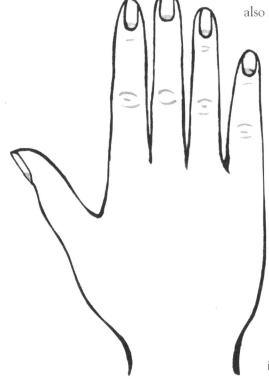

True lovers of beauty, people with conic hands are often found gracing art galleries, antique stores, or botanic gardens. They are likely to have beautifully decorated homes, filled with gorgeous pieces of art, and tend to see big bunches of flowers as a household necessity rather than an extravagance.

The conic hand denotes creativity; a large number of artists, writers, musicians, and actors have this type of hand. However, the main downfall of these people can be their inability to carry a project through. They may start off brimming with enthusiasm, but soon lose interest and move on to the next thing that catches their interest.

If the fingers on the conic hand have knotty joints (prominent knuckles that bulge), the person will be quite the philosopher, with an innate need to discover every possible thing about any subject of interest. You are likely to find this person at the library or possibly in college, working on her second, third, or fourth degree.

The person with the conic hand has a love of all things sensual: food, surroundings, and sex. This can be a downfall, particularly if the **line of escape** (see page 75) is evident, or the mount of Venus dominates (see pages 86–87). But a conic-handed person with a palm that is firm, with well-formed lines, will keep these passions in check and the intellect will rule.

 WORKBOOK EXERCISES FOR THE CONIC–HANDED

1. To help boost positive qualities and diminish negative qualities, conic-handed individuals should spend a few minutes each day reflecting on the following:
   - I am strong and disciplined.
   - I am organized and able to fulfill any task.
   - I accept order and discipline in my life.
2. List five personal qualities that you feel enrich your life.
3. List five qualities you'd like to nurture in yourself.
4. Compose a ten-point plan of how you can use your strengths to help turn your weaknesses into positive attributes. What are three concrete steps that you can take today? How can you incorporate these steps into your everyday life?

THE SPATULATE HAND

A spatulate hand may have a palm that is broad, square, or narrow, but the one defining characteristic is the fingers that splay out at the tip much like a spatula. Alternatively, the palms may have the appearance of a shovel—narrow at one end and broad at the other. People with spatulate hands are highly active, rarely spending any time at rest. They use even their "leisure" time actively, participating in a wide range of activities.

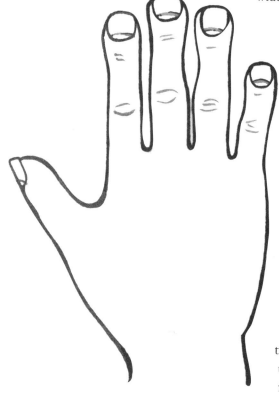

People with spatulate hands tend to be very confident of their abilities, and this, combined with innovative and energetic minds, can lead to great success. Entrepreneurs tend to have spatulate hands, and this hand type is quite common in the finance sector and the advertising world as well.

Spending time with people with spatulate hands will never be boring. Their lives are full and they are dynamic, interesting, and excitable. They have an amazing ability to infect others with their enthusiasm and therefore make great team leaders. When spatulate types have square palms, you will find they tend to be very practical and grounded, despite unconventional appearances that are often to the contrary. Whatever happens, they can usually manage to effect a fortunate outcome for themselves regardless of how dire the situation may appear.

When a spatulate hand is too flexible, this indicates that hedonistic pleasures may take precedence over work. Caution should be exercised to keep check on wild behavior. Also, examine the mount of Venus (see pages 86–87) and the heart line (see pages 44–45) for other indications of an overly passionate nature.

The spatulate hand is the hand of the do-it-yourself fanatic. People with hands of this shape tend to be skilled at creating things with their hands. In fact, the manual dexterity of spatulate-handed people may be exceptional, and they may be ingenious inventors.

 WORKBOOK EXERCISES FOR THE SPATULATE-HANDED

1. To help boost positive qualities and diminish negative qualities, spatulate-handed individuals should spend a few minutes per day reflecting on the following:
   • I feel complete.
   • Balance in my life is spent at rest along with activity.
   • I set aside time to tune out the world.
2. List five personal qualities that you feel enrich your life.
3. List five qualities you'd like to nurture in yourself.
4. Compose a ten-point plan of how you can use your strengths to help turn your weaknesses into positive attributes. What are three concrete steps that you can take today? How can you incorporate these steps into your everyday life?

THE PSYCHIC HAND

This hand type is as rare as it is pretty. The palm is long and slender, and the fingers too are long and graceful, with delicate, pointed tips. Psychic hands are similar to conic hands in that the owners have a love of beauty; however, due to their extreme sensitivity, those with psychic hands tend to be rather high-strung.

As evidenced by the name, people with psychic hands are very intuitive and are often psychic. This skill can range from acute attunement to body language and the nuances of speech patterns to actual clairvoyance.

Highly creative and imaginative, people with psychic hands are artistic, but may have trouble coping with daily life. They tend to be a little out of place in the everyday world and need to surround themselves with practical people who can help them deal with mundane matters.

People with these hands are often artists, hairstylists, or beauticians—areas where they can work on achieving their ideal of beauty. In times gone by, women with these hands would be "kept women," with their male benefactors attending to the practicalities.

Psychic hands tend to be pale, with a fine skin texture, and the thumb is usually long and flexible. The lines on this hand are not strong or deeply etched and, depending on how sensitive the person is, can be covered in a crosshatch of lines.

People with psychic hands are often highly empathetic and may need to avoid watching upsetting images on the nightly news in order to maintain an even balance. They also need to avoid spending their time immersed in the atrocities of this world. As people with psychic hands have an interest in spiritual matters, they may find that daily meditation can help ground them and make life more livable.

 WORKBOOK EXERCISES FOR THE PSYCHIC–HANDED

1. To help boost positive qualities and diminish negative qualities, psychic-handed individuals should spend a few minutes per day reflecting on the following:
   - I am calm.
   - I feel safe and content with my life.
   - I accept that I have complete confidence in my abilities.
2. List five personal qualities that you feel enrich your life.
3. List five qualities you'd like to nurture in yourself.
4. Compose a ten-point plan of how you can use your strengths to help turn your weaknesses into positive attributes. What are three concrete steps that you can take today? How can you incorporate these steps into your everyday life?

THE MIXED HAND

Not every hand fits neatly into one of the categories of hand types discussed in this chapter. For this reason, the mixed hand forms a classification of its own.

A true mixed hand contains two or more of the classifications of the previous hand types. Hence you may find a hand that appears conic but has a few spatulate fingers along with the conic ones. Alternatively, the palm may seem square, yet the hand may have conic, psychic, or spatulate fingers.

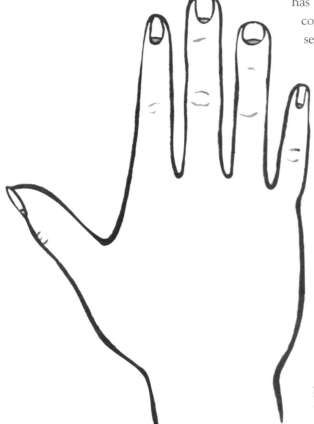

Generally speaking, those with mixed hands are adaptable and flexible. They may seem adept at anything they put their minds to and may be jacks-of-all-trades. These people mix well with others, as they can easily slot into any group of people, subtly adapting to the mood of the crowd.

When you read a hand of the mixed type, it is important to take into consideration its dominant features and then ascertain what the other features are trying to tell you. You will need to look at the individual parts of the hand before making any assumptions. The following chapters in this book will help you with this, particularly when it comes to making judgments about the fingers and the thumb. You can be certain of one thing about people with mixed hands: they are eclectic individuals with some very interesting characteristics.

 WORKBOOK EXERCISES FOR THE MIXED–HANDED

1. To help boost positive qualities and diminish negative qualities, mixed-handed individuals should spend a few minutes per day reflecting on the following:
   • I am a well-balanced individual.
   • I know exactly what I want.
   • I accept the right to be me.
2. List five personal qualities that you feel enrich your life.
3. List five qualities you'd like to nurture in yourself.
4. Compose a ten-point plan of how you can use your strengths to help turn your weaknesses into positive attributes. What are three concrete steps that you can take today? How can you incorporate these steps into your everyday life?

REVIEW

Studying palmistry will make you familiar with the five basic categories of hand shapes and the other features of the hand. You can judge a lot about a person by the hand shape. When doing a reading, keep referring back to this shape. The characteristics of the basic shapes are:

- **square hand**: practical, structured, and ordered
- **conic hand**: artistic, intuitive, and enthusiastic
- **spatulate hand**: active, entrepreneurial, and grounded
- **psychic hand**: idealistic, impressionable, and spiritual
- **mixed hand**: versatile, adaptable, and likable

Aside from the shape of the hand, other factors should be considered when reading a person's palm:

- The **flexibility** of the hand—a moderately flexible hand signifies a balanced individual who is well adapted to society and is able to relate to a wide range of people.
- **Skin texture**—fine and coarse skin indicate different temperaments: more refined and more insensitive, respectively.
- **Hand color** points to state of health and well-being. Note if the skin is pale and bluish, pink, red, or gray, and what this can indicate.

When you first start reading palms, you may find it difficult to determine the different characteristics. This will become easier over time; the best way is to practice as much as possible. Observe the hands of everyone you see and try to isolate the dominant features. You will soon find that observing hands is both compulsive and revealing.

WORKBOOK EXERCISES

1. Before attempting to look at anyone else's palm, take the time to identify your own.

2. Once you have done this, it is time to move on and try to identify another individual's hand type. Take photocopies or prints of the hands of five of your friends or family members. Try not to use only family members as subjects, as you may find that many similarities will recur. Using a ruler and a pen and the copied image of the palm, draw a line around each of the palm's four sides. Now, looking at the formation you have drawn, identify the shape of the palm. For example, is it square, with all four sides of an equal length? Or perhaps conic, tapering at the top or the bottom?

3. Examine each of the fingers. What is their length in relation to the palm? Fingers that are approximately as long as the palm are considered to be of normal length, but when assessing this, first ascertain if the palm itself seems unnaturally long. If it is, then the fingers may still be considered long even though they are shorter than the palm. Ask:
   - Are the fingers straight or knotty? (See also page 116.)
   - Are the fingertips rounded, pointed, flat, or spatulate?
   - Is there more than one finger type on the hand? (See also page 115.)

4. Now, looking at the hand itself, rather than the copied image, note the following:
   - skin color
   - skin texture
   - flexibility

5. Take all these points into consideration and then categorize each of the five hands you have copied.
   - Which shape category do they fall into?
   - How well do they fit into the personality types outlined in this chapter?
   - What about your own hand?

Once you have mastered the art of being able to assess the categories of hand shape, you will be ready to move on to the next step—the primary lines on the palm.

CHAPTER THREE

THE PRIMARY LINES

Discover the primary lines of the palm and their significant meanings.
Learn to read these lines and their special features.

When someone thrusts a palm toward you, eager to have it read, it is almost inevitable that one of the first questions will be, "How long will I live?" People who know little else about palmistry will know there is a life line on the palm and will assume it can give evidence of life expectancy. However, while the life line *can* be an indication of the length of life, your subjects need to know that they can gain very different information from this marking. Many features on the palm could indicate the subject's possible life span, but all are highly changeable and should never be commented upon. Tell your subject that a short life line does not mean he is likely to die by his thirtieth birthday, nor does a long life line guarantee extreme longevity.

Palms vary a great deal in the markings they contain, but virtually every palm will have the four primary lines etched upon it. These are:

- the **life line**
- the **heart line**
- the **head line**
- the **fate line**

Some hands, in particular the square hand, will seem rather empty, often having the basic lines but few others. On some other palms, it will be difficult to find the primary lines, as the palms will be covered in a variety of lines.

RIGHT OR LEFT?

When it comes to performing a reading, you may wonder whether to read the right or the left hand. The answer is both, because each hand will tell you something different. Each person has an **active hand** and a **passive hand**. The active hand is the one we use most—for writing and for using tools and implements. For a left-handed person, therefore, the left hand is the active one, and the opposite is true for a right-handed person. If someone claims to be ambidextrous, you may need to question this person more closely to find which hand he prefers to use. For example, some older people may have been born left-handed and forced to write with their right hand, but still use the left hand on a daily basis. Therefore, you would classify this person as ambidextrous, but consider the left hand dominant.

The passive hand reveals our destiny, or what life has planned for us, while the active hand shows what we have made of our life. Some people have markings that are almost identical on both hands, indicating that they have followed their destiny to the letter. Others may have two very different palms. Someone who has similar markings on the active and passive hands has been content with what fate has dealt out. Palmists look at both hands when reading, looking to the active hand to see the way the subject is living his life and to the passive hand to explain how life could be lived differently.

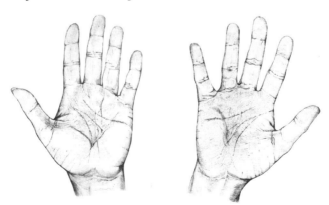

A person's active hand is their dominant hand—usually the one used for writing.

SPECIAL MARKINGS

When assessing the primary lines, look for these markings, which have a similar meaning regardless of the line on which they appear.

ISLANDS

These are disturbances, but not breaks, in lines and appear as irregularly shaped ovals within the line. They indicate a weakness or a time of turmoil at a particular point in the person's life when he was not completely focused on his goals. An **island** that appears on the life line can indicate that the subject will suffer a period of illness that will incapacitate him in some way. Islands on the heart line indicate emotional upheaval and will often appear at the stage when a relationship is in trouble.

CHAINS

These are a series of islands joined together. They often occur at the beginning of lines and reveal the turmoil or period of upheaval—the sense of being pulled in many directions—which the subject endured while trying to work through a difficult situation. Our childhood is usually indicated by **chains**, as we take numerous paths in order to become an adult. In fact, it is common for many lines, particularly the life line and the heart line, to start chained, as it is during our youth that we are often subject to emotional upheaval.

DOTS

These are colored indentations on a line. They can appear on the palm in a variety of colors and on any line or mount. They normally indicate a setback of some kind or a period of upheaval. On the life line, a dot would mean a physical upset, such as a sickness; on the heart line, it denotes emotional trauma; and on the fate line it is usually indicative of a period when the subject is questioning his direction in life.

GRILLES

These are a series of crisscrossed minor lines on the palm. **Grilles** are usually quite fine and indicate a stage of disorientation when energy was weakened, or a period of frustration, such as a time when the subject has dived into a situation without thinking and faced difficulty as a result. For example, a busy person may agree to take on more work without considering how to achieve his goals, and may become overworked or stressed as a result.

FORKS

If a line ends in two or three branches, these branches form a fork. Forks are considered a good sign, particularly when found at the end of one of the **major lines**. They can also balance different traits. For example, if the head line ends in a fork, this can mean that the subject's impetuousness is tempered with caution. The triple fork, or **trident**, is considered the most fortunate ending for the heart line, as it is considered that the person will be a romantic with a realistic base—someone with the best of all possible attitudes toward love.

SQUARES

These indicate a form of protection and are a particularly fortuitous formation when they appear around a break in a line. The protection may come in the form of luck, or even as a guardian angel, either living or dead. It is normally a good idea to take any sign of a **square** positively, but sometimes the square can indicate a period of confinement or even a spell of imprisonment when it occurs on the life line where there is no break. Squares on **travel lines** indicate protection from harm when traveling.

SPLITS OR SPLINTERS

If a line splinters or splits, this means its energy is weakened. Often, this occurs when a person takes a different path in life from what fate offered, or from the way he had been living. Romantic upsets can cause splinters in the heart line. Those hurt by a lover may change their romantic inclinations and could even become more practical in matters of the heart. Splits in the fate line are not uncommon and are usually indicative of a change in career.

THE LIFE LINE

The life line begins at the edge of the palm, between the index finger and thumb, and curves its way around the mount of Venus to end somewhere near the base of the palm. Any major event in life, physical or emotional, is found on the life line. It reveals our vitality and endurance and can also give us some idea of our expected life span.

Looking at the life line in isolation does not reveal how long we will live—other factors need to be considered as well. We cannot just assume that a long life line means a long life. The reverse may be true if there are other indications in the palm, particularly if it is the palm of a daredevil. And a short life line does not mean a short life—particularly if the subject is robust and healthy. When assessing the life line, it is important to look at the active hand, not the passive hand, particularly if the two lines are of differing lengths.

The life line also indicates the current state of mind of the subject. The lines on the active palm are in a continual state of flux, changing as the state of mind changes. For example, if the subject is feeling depressed, this will show in a weak, short, broken life line, possibly ending in a **bar** (a short line perpendicular to the life line: $\overset{\times}{\underset{\times}{\times}}$). Should you be alarmed by such findings, it is best to be as reassuring and positive as possible. You could also advise the subject to seek help from a professional or to speak to a trusted friend or family member. The life line will strengthen once a person in difficulties such as these has had treatment. If this person gains help with serious problems, his outlook may change and the life line may then be strengthened.

TIMING ON THE LIFE LINE

When you are evaluating a life line, divide it into thirds, starting at the point where it begins between the thumb and the index finger. The first third shows childhood, the second adulthood, and the final third maturity. The best life line is long, deep, and unbroken. This indicates a person with vitality, stamina, and a healthy outlook on life. A line that is short but still deep and strong is also good, as it indicates the kind of healthy disposition needed to overcome any obstacles and have a long, healthy life.

When reading a palm, you should never, regardless of what you see, predict a person's death. If you see a potential health problem (see later in this chapter), you could advise the subject to watch his diet, keep stress under control, and exercise often, but a negative reading is beneficial to no one.

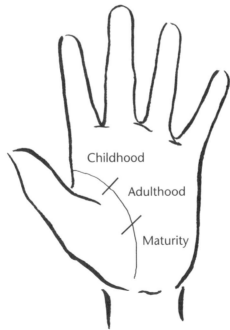

SPECIAL FEATURES OF THE LIFE LINE

When the life line is thin, broken, or heavily chained, this can indicate a person with a weak disposition. The person may be unhealthy or just unsuited to dealing with the situations that arise in everyday life. Changing a poor diet can see a life line becoming much stronger, along with its owner.

If one or two lines run inside and parallel to the life line, this is known as a double or triple life line. A formation like this indicates special protection in life and extra vitality, and indicates that this person will be blessed with good luck and a long, healthy life.

A life line that swoops out broadly in a wide arc indicates a person with high self-esteem, someone who is determined to make a success of himself. Conversely, a line that clings to the thumb shows an insecure person who constantly feels that he measures up negatively against others.

Sometimes a life line will appear to be short, but on closer inspection a separate life line will be found starting nearby. This is difficult to assess and can often be mistaken for a fate line. If this configuration is found, it reveals a person who has split away from his earlier self. For example, this person may have had a difficult childhood and may then have broken away, becoming a completely different person.

A straight life line is normally found on those who have little belief in themselves. It is the sign of a follower rather than a doer.

If the line curves and ends under the thumb, the person will have a very active old age. A life line that crosses the palm and ends on the **mount of Luna** (see pages 84–85) on the opposite side of the palm shows a person whose love of travel will rule his life. Often, such a person will travel most of the time and will settle in far-off places.

The ideal life line is one that is strong and well formed, curving well around the base of the thumb and ending near the wrist; one that is free from breaks, islands, and **lines of influence**. It is well defined, yet not too deeply etched.

Occasionally, you may find a person without a life line. This is very rare and is usually the result of a life-threatening incident. Some accidents and health problems can cause lines on the palms to disappear, but they will normally reappear once health is regained.

MARKINGS ON THE LIFE LINE

A life line that is chained at the beginning indicates problems in childhood. These problems may be either emotional or physical. When a life line is chained for its entire length, this means that the person has poor health.

Islands on the life line indicate a period of trauma. This may mean that the person has been hospitalized or that there is a period of emotional upheaval at the time indicated. Islands can reveal incidents in both the past and the future.

A square on the life line is a sign of protection. At the stage in life indicated, someone was, or will be, looking out for the subject.

Lines of influence are short lines that rise up from or cross the life line. These can show moments when the person has had to triumph over adversity. Short lines that head down from the life line have a negative implication. At this time the person has not had the energy to overcome concerns and worries, and has allowed the negative aspects of life to get the better of him.

The **line of escape** (also known as the poison line) runs straight across the base of the palm from the mount of Venus to the mount of Luna. It can be negative, as it is indicative of a person who runs away from problems instead of dealing with them. This person may also seek solace in drugs as a way of escaping difficulties.

The life line reveals how we are coping with life and the unexpected challenges it produces for us. If the middle section of the life line is weakened, this can show that we are not coping, or will not cope, with the changes that wrought our lives in middle age. This is an indication that we need to work on strengthening our self-esteem and discovering our true inner nature.

The line of escape

43

THE HEART LINE

The heart line is placed high on the palm, and starts on the outer side, under the little finger. It moves across the palm, ending somewhere near the index finger. The heart line is often the darkest line on the palm; if this line appears significantly darker than the others, it is likely that the subject has emotional problems or is suffering from poor health in the areas of the heart or circulation.

The heart line reveals our emotions and how we deal with others. It can show how we react romantically, but it can also indicate how we relate to friends and relatives. It is often interesting to compare the heart lines on the active and passive hands. Most heart lines will reveal weaknesses and upsets in the form of chains and islands, particularly in the teenage years and early twenties. Some people react to these upsets in a dramatic manner; they may try to ensure that they never experience such hurts again by completely changing their romantic style. Such people may have heart lines with a passionate broad curve on the passive hand, while the active hand has a straighter heart line, indicating a more cautious view of relationships.

MARKINGS AND SPECIAL FEATURES

The ideal heart line runs almost completely across the palm, is smooth and free of breaks, and ends in a triple-forked formation. If this trident appears, an equilibrium of the emotions is present in the individual: passion is balanced with common sense and sentimentality. A double fork is also positive, as it also reveals balance.

A long heart line (one that ends under the index finger) reveals the ability to give and receive love. If the line is short, however, emotional blockages will cause the subject to have difficulty falling in love, and this person will feel unworthy and unable to accept the love of others. Such a person will need to work on self-esteem in order to gain the belief that he is capable of loving and being loved.

A clear, unblemished heart line is very unusual. A person with such a line will have managed to have a straightforward love life, free of heartache and problems—a very rare individual indeed. Breaks on the heart line indicate breakups and emotional disturbances in relationships. Islands on the heart line can indicate health problems if they are underneath the **mount of Mercury**. If they are elsewhere on the line, they are indicative of a time of confusion or mourning in that period.

If a heart line is doubled (if it has a sister line directly above or below it), this means double protection in aspects of love. The person with this marking is likely to be very committed and faithful in his relationships. A person with a shallow heart line, in contrast, will tend to be shallow in his relationships. Such a person will often be quite uninvolved emotionally and will often have purely physical relationships.

CURVES AND STRAIGHT LINES

When the heart line swoops upward with a dramatic flourish, you see before you a person with an intensely passionate nature. Such a person will fall in love quickly and heavily, but will be quick to get over it and move on to the next person, with a shrug of the shoulders when the relationship runs its course. A straight heart line, however, indicates a realist. Such a person will be wary of falling in love, but when he does so the commitment will be long-lasting. When this subject's heart breaks, he will be totally devastated and will mourn for an extended period before warily moving on to the next relationship.

When a straight heart line is set high on the palm close to the base of the fingers, this usually indicates a person who is cold and unemotional. A high head line reinforces this quality.

The area between the head and the heart lines is known as the **great quadrangle**. A narrow gap between these two lines indicates a person with a narrow mind—the broader the space, the broader the mind.

Curved heart line

Straight heart line

Broad gap in quadrangle

Narrow gap in quadrangle

HAND SHAPE AND THE HEART LINE

When looking at the heart line, you will need to take into consideration the shape of the hand. For example, a square hand usually contains a straight heart line, but if this line is curved, the subject is more likely to suffer extreme disappointment in love than someone with a curved line on another hand shape. People with square hands and curved heart lines are likely to be so upset by a slight that they will brood on it for years and allow it to have a major effect on their relationships.

People with conic hands tend to have curved heart lines. These people are affectionate and demonstrative, the type of people who are inclined to be very dramatic and thoughtful in both gestures and actions. A friend who turns up bearing your favorite flowers on your birthday is likely to be a conic-handed person with a curved heart line.

People with conic hands and straight heart lines are more inclined to keep their feelings to themselves. They also have a tendency to be jealous and possessive in relationships, and need to learn to express their feelings if they are to have successful relationships.

SPECIAL MARKINGS

- A **star** on the heart line underneath the index finger indicates a successful marriage or life partnership.

- Islands on the heart line indicate periods of depression or unhappiness, often linked to a breakup of a relationship.

- Lines of influence rising from the heart line indicate happiness in relationships.

- Downward lines reveal testing times that caused a setback in the subject's life.

- Chains are present on the heart line if the subject has had emotional problems.

HEALTH ON THE HEART LINE

There are many health conditions that can be read on the heart line, vascular problems being one of these. When a heart line is made up of a series of chains or seems frayed in appearance, this indicates that there are potential problems with the vascular system and attention needs to be paid to the subject's health.

However, it is important not to consider the heart line as a sole entity. Also, look at the color of the skin, the fingernails, and the skin texture as pointers. Nails and skin that are healthy and pink are a good sign; those with a purple or bluish tinge are not. A coarse skin texture can also indicate problems with circulation.

When the heart line is shallow and faint, health problems are likely to be caused by the emotions or the mental state, whereas this is unlikely in those with a deeply etched heart line. Their problems are more likely to be of a physical nature.

When reading the heart line, remember to compare the lines on the active and the passive hands, as it is here that you are likely to find differences. They will show the effect that previous relationships have had on this person: he may have been hurt in a previous relationship and has become less emotional in all relationships, or the opposite may be true.

A NOTE REGARDING HEALTH

One of the most positive things about palmistry is that you have the power to effect change. When you see signs on your hand that may signify potential health problems, you can be pleased to note that they occur to advise you and help you make the right lifestyle choices for optimum physical and mental health.

When you do note signs of ill health on your palm, first take a step back and make notes on where you can simplify your everyday existence. Simply saying no to things you can't possibly take on, or don't really want to do, can actually be one of the most positive steps you can take. If you learn to assert your rights as an individual and do what is best for yourself, you will find that it spills over into other areas of your life, and besides yourself, your friends, family, and coworkers will benefit from a new, happier you.

THE SIMIAN LINE

On some palms, instead of distinct heart and head lines there is only one line running across the palm. This is called the **simian line**. It is relatively rare.

There are a lot of myths surrounding the simian line, one of these being that it is a sign of mental retardation and is an indicator of Down syndrome. This is not true. People born with Down syndrome are no more likely to have a simian line than any other person.

The person with a simian line is usually a very stubborn individual. The heart is likely to rule the head, or vice versa. Things are always black or white with this person—there are no half-measures.

This subject's career is often at risk, as emotions will often cause difficulty at work—such a person may be unable to separate himself from any situation, reacting negatively and taking every issue personally.

There may also be problems in relationships, as people with the simian line may be extremely passionate one day and cool and detached the next, leaving partners in a state of confusion.

Nobody knows what causes the fusion of the head and heart lines, but some people have hypothesized that this is the result of some kind of emotional shock. Interestingly, people with simian lines have difficulty dealing with stress and may react with hysterics or go to bed with severe migraines when everything gets too hard to deal with.

THE HEAD LINE

Contrary to popular opinion, the head line does not indicate intelligence, but it does reveal how we use our intellect. This is the line that cuts across the middle of the palm, underneath the heart line. It starts from one of three positions: high on the palm on the **mount of Jupiter** (see page 90), attached to the life line, or inside the life line.

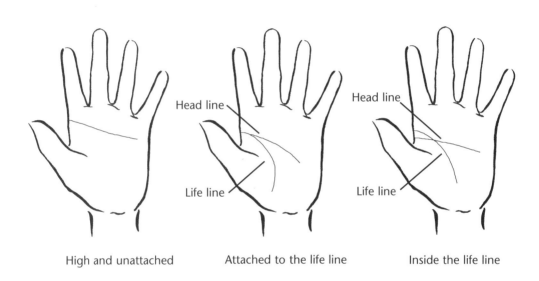

High and unattached   Attached to the life line   Inside the life line

WHERE IT BEGINS

When the head line starts high on the palm, this indicates a high achiever. When the line is long, clear, and attached at some point to the life line, the person is destined to be the boss. Such a person will be enthusiastic and determined, and when there is a slight curve to the line, endowed with creative flair. This creativity will be balanced by a sense of caution, with little regard for their associates. They may also be foolhardy, rushing into new projects without considering the possible dangers.

When the head line is connected at the start to the life line, this reveals a sensitive and cautious individual, often unduly concerned with the opinions of others and how he appears to them. People with these markings need encouragement to let go occasionally and follow their first impulses rather than fretting over what is the best thing to do.

When the head line begins within the life line, this is an indication that the subject is a worrier, particularly if the mount of Mars (see pages 88–89), where it begins, is flat. If the mount is rounded, then the subject will have the ability to overcome almost any difficulty.

If a head line is very high on the palm—so much so that there is barely any space between the heart line and the head line—this indicates that the intellect will rule the emotions. However, the opposite will be true if the heart line is the stronger of the two.

When the head line crosses the palm completely from one side to the other, this is known as the **Sydney line**. This line shares many similarities with the simian line (see page 49), but the heart line is present on the hand.

CURVES AND STRAIGHT LINES

Ideally, the head line should be long and strong, with a slight curve in the middle or toward the end. A generally straight line with a curve is indicative of a person whose creativity is tempered with practicality. The straighter the line, the more practical the person, and the more curved the line, the more creative. A head line that travels straight across the palm indicates a person who sees things in black and white. Such a person would be good at following instructions, but would not like being called on to come up with creative solutions. Once again, however, it is important when assessing the shape of the head line to take the hand shape into consideration. For example, you would expect to see a curved head line on a conic hand, but this would be more remarkable on a square hand.

A strongly drawn head line that continues far across the palm indicates a person with an enormous capacity for knowledge and someone who is using that ability to its fullest extent. Conversely, if a head line is weak and short (anything that takes up less than a quarter of the palm's width), this indicates that the person is not using his full intellectual ability. People who are content with themselves would be expected to have a strong head line.

THE END OF THE LINE

When a long, moderately curved head line ends in a fork on the mount of Luna, the person will have a creative ability with words—this formation is often called the **writer's fork**. The deeper into Luna the head line ends, the more frequently the person will retreat into imaginary worlds. This is particularly the case if the head line is also deeply curved. Caution needs to be exercised to ensure that this person has a dose of reality every now and again.

An unusual termination of the head line involves an upward swing, with the line ending on the mount of Mars. With this configuration, you can be assured that the subject will achieve unusual success as a result of their intellect. This person really values money and can be very hard on his employees.

MARKINGS ON THE LINE

A break in the head line shows that the person has made a complete change in direction. Look to see if the head line is linked at the start to the life line. If so, this reveals that family influences have played a strong role in this individual's development; however, when the person was ready, he broke free and turned personal dreams into reality.

An island on the head line reveals a weakening of this line. If it occurs early on the line, the person can often move on from any difficulties, but when it is at the end it may be harder for the person to recover, so early intervention is required to help halt any difficulties.

A double head line is very rare, but when you do come across one you have met a person of great intelligence who is able to work on a range of subjects and still do them justice.

People who have a head line that is chained, wavy, or weak may be unable to concentrate on any single thing for a significant period of time. Such people may also have a low boredom threshold, mainly because they find little that can maintain their interest. When the line wavers over the palm, you may find that the person is unable to make decisions and is incapable of fulfilling any long-term goals.

Thin lines indicate a person who lacks staying power. Such a person would be an exceptional worker in short bursts, but will need different projects in order to maintain interest over any period.

However, just like any other line on the palms, the head line can be strengthened once a weakness is identified and a plan put in place to overcome any problems. Structures implemented to help with organization, study undertaken to increase the intellect, and exercises performed to increase self-esteem can all help to set a subject on the path to success.

TIMING ON THE HEAD LINE

To time an event on the head line, start your measurement on the inside of the palm, between the thumb and index finger. Now, starting from this point, divide the line into three: birth to twenty years, twenty to fifty years, and fifty years onward.

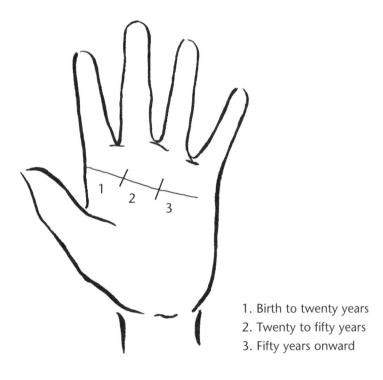

1. Birth to twenty years
2. Twenty to fifty years
3. Fifty years onward

THE FATE LINE

The fate line runs up the center of the palm, from the wrist up to the middle, or Saturn, finger (see page 118). This line may not be present on all hands or may be present only on one hand. It reveals what we are making of our lives and the directions in which we are heading. The fate line also indicates how content we are with our choices. For example, a long, strong fate line is normally found on a person who is quite happy with his job, level of success, and—most importantly—with life in general.

Just as with the other lines, you need to consider the hand shape before making any assessment of the fate line. In fact, this is probably more vital for the fate line than for any other. Psychic-shaped hands tend to have smaller, less defined, and shorter fate lines than the conic, spatulate, or mixed hand shapes. A long, strong fate line on a square hand would be considered quite remarkable and indicative of a person who is destined for great success and satisfaction.

While the fate line usually starts at the base of the palm and continues upward to the **Saturn finger**, there are a number of variations of this line, making it difficult to identify on some palms—particularly busy ones. The line of fate can arise from the mount of Luna, the line of life, the head line, or even the heart line. Bear in mind, though, that it is considered one of the four major lines and as such should be stronger than other minor lines and of a similar strength to the other lines mentioned in this chapter.

The lack of a fate line can indicate a person who

has not yet found his direction in life. Many children do not have a fate line and it is not uncommon for the fate line to form only when a person is in their teens or twenties. If a fate line never forms, this can indicate a person who is never quite sure that what he is doing is the correct thing.

WHERE IT BEGINS

While the line of fate can start down near the wrist, it is not uncommon for this line to start higher on the palm, indicating a person who finds his true vocation later in life. When a fate line is joined to the life line, it indicates that the subject's family will play a major role in the direction that the person takes. This is the kind of line you would expect to find on a person who is, for example, one of a long line of doctors. The position where the fate line breaks away from the life line indicates where the person will break away, or has broken away, from the influence of the family.

The fate line that starts at the wrist indicates a person who was destined from birth to live the life he is living. It is not usual for this line to be consistently strong. Often, the line starts off a little weak and tends to waver, indicating the different directions in which the person may consider heading.

If the fate line starts at the head line, you can be assured that this person spent a great deal of time thinking about his direction in life before coming to a decision. This direction will be governed by the intellect.

People with a fate line starting at the heart line have love governing their lives. Any decisions about life's direction will come quite late in life, but they will be passionate and enjoy every moment of what they do.

A fate line that originates in the mount of Luna could indicate that success is ultimately due to the will of other people. For example, the subject may be a politician or an actor; no matter how determined or talented this person is, ultimately success will depend on being chosen by others.

SPECIAL FEATURES

Breaks and islands in the fate line indicate that the person will have ups and downs in their careers, and that success will often be tempered with failure. A long, straight fate line, free from any breaks or chains, indicates a person who is likely to stay in the same profession from the time of leaving school until retirement.

When the line branches off, this can reveal success in more than one area. If there is a complete break, a new avenue will be tried; if it is just a small branch on an unbroken line, then this person may have success in an area similar to his usual occupation.

When the fate line is the dominant line on the hand, this can reveal a person who puts far too much energy into work, to the detriment of all other areas of his life.

A square on a fate line is a fortuitous sign, indicating protection from misfortune.

THE END OF THE LINE

A fate line may run right up the palm and end somewhere on the middle, or Saturn, finger. This reveals a person who just does not know when to stop. This type of line is likely to be found on the hand of an entertainer who continues his career long after the adulation of the public has run out.

When the fate line ends on a mount, success is indicated in the area defined by that mount. A fate line that ends on the mount of Jupiter foreshadows great and unusual success. Subjects with this configuration are ambitious, talented, and determined. For further information, see Chapter Five to learn about what each mount governs.

TIMING ON THE HAND

It can be difficult to pinpoint on a hand exactly the time when an event has occurred or will occur in our lives, but it is quite easy to give a time frame of events once you have become practiced at reading palms. A palmist who is able to give an exact date probably has psychic abilities; other palmists, however, can make a fairly accurate measurement when using copies of the palms and a ruler or protractor to measure a line.

When figuring out timing on the hand, start at the beginning of the line and divide it into thirds: birth to twenty years, twenty to fifty years, and fifty years onward.

Assessing time on the fate line is different. The section from the start of the line until it meets the head line represents a person's life up to the age of thirty-five. The remainder of the line after this point represents the person's life after thirty-five. Time on the fate line is measured in this way because most of us do not have a clear idea of who we are and what we want to do until we are at least this age. That said, it is not uncommon to encounter an individual who is still finding his way beyond this age. You will, in fact, find that for some people the fate line does not even start until the head line or beyond, indicating a person who does not find his own way until later in life.

By dividing up the fate line, it is easy to see what effect certain events have played on an individual. A person who always wanted to fly as a child and grew up to become a pilot will have a straight, unwavering fate line. The youth who did not decide what he wanted to do with his life until in his mid-twenties or thirties will have a fate line marked by a series of branches, breaks, and loosely woven chains.

Assessing time on the fate line is different from other lines.
1. Birth to thirty-five years
2. Thirty-five years onward

REVIEW

Virtually every hand you read will contain the four primary lines in some form. From these lines you will be able to gather a great deal of information about people—their lust for life, their relations with others, their desire for success, and how well they are using their intellectual abilities. The four lines have distinct meanings:

- The **life line** reveals how robust we are and how well we accept the challenges life casts before us.
- The **heart line** shows the passionate side of our nature and how we deal with our relationships.
- The **head line** shows how we think and indicates our intellectual skills.
- The **fate line** shows how well we will succeed in our chosen career and the path that we will follow.

Some hands will not have the head line and the heart line but will have a formation known as the simian line. A person with this formation may be very stubborn.

Certain markings usually appear on the four main lines and it is important to take these into consideration when doing a reading. The method for judging timing, as outlined in this chapter, helps us assess whether the markings occur early, in the middle, or later in life, and what this means for the subject.

When you first start doing readings for enjoyment (this is how most palmists begin), you will certainly be able to gain enough understanding of other people's characters from these lines and from their hand shape to gain insight into their lives. Keep your readings upbeat and light, concentrating on the positive aspects of your subjects' hands. Even by looking at the major lines alone, you will be able to find something positive to comment upon—an essential for the practice of palmistry.

WORKBOOK EXERCISES

Answer questions 1–4 in your journal for each of the primary lines.

1. What does this line represent for me?

2. What are five aspirations you hold for each line (for example, for the life line: "I wish to lead a creative life.")?

3. List in order of importance—with one being the most important—what each of these mean to you: life challenges, passion and relationships, intellectual stimulation, and destiny and success.

4. What do the answers to questions 1–3 tell you about your feelings associated with each of the primary lines? How do you think a reading may be positively or negatively affected by your personal beliefs? For example, if you don't believe in fate, how would you read the differences between the passive and active hands?

5. Make photocopies or prints of palms of a few people you know reasonably well (so that you can tell how accurate your assessment has been once you have completed it), and for each handprint answer the following questions about each of the primary lines.
   - Is this the dominant line on the hand?
   - Are the lines deeply etched, finely drawn, or normal?
   - Are there any markings on the lines?
   - Where do the lines start and end?
   - Do the lines end in an unusual formation (e.g., a trident)?

6. Now, reading back over the chapter, see what these lines tell you about your subject and make notes about what you have found.
   - Does your view change when you add the factor of the subject's hand shape?
   - By comparing the fate line and the head line, can you gain an understanding of the type of career that would suit your subject?
   - What do you understand about the subject after examining each of the primary lines?

7. Does your analysis fit with what you know about this person?

CHAPTER FOUR

THE SECONDARY LINES

What are the secondary lines on the palm? How do they affect a reading?
Learn the meaning of these lines.

Once you have learned the importance of the primary lines, it is time to move on to the other features on the palm. Reading the secondary lines uncovers the subject's individual interests and talents, and this will help to refine your reading. The secondary lines also have different meanings when considered in conjunction with the shape of the fingers and the palm. With palmistry it is best to not consider merely one feature at a time—you should constantly refer to other features before making any decisions on the relevance of any part of the hand.

It is not unusual to find a hand without any secondary lines. A small minority of hands contain only three lines, usually the heart, head, and life lines. This is called an **empty hand**; you would probably be correct in assuming that the subject is very content with life at the moment and desires nothing more than the basic pleasures. The empty hand is more typical of the square-handed individual than of people with other hand shapes and would actually be quite remarkable if found on another hand type, particularly the conic and the psychic hands.

The identity of the secondary lines can be difficult to assess. The hand may be covered in lines—the hand of the person who is never at rest, the person who is constantly thinking about new things, worrying and fretting about what to do next, and barely concentrating on the task at hand. It is important to be careful when deciding on the nature of a secondary line. Also, pay particular attention to where the line begins and ends, and how deeply it is etched on a palm—the darker a line, the more important the impact of that aspect of life on the individual.

THE ACTIVE AND PASSIVE HANDS

When assessing the secondary lines, pay attention to both the active and the passive hands; you will often see widely divergent tales on the two hands. A palm may contain a secondary line on the passive but not the active hand. This is an indication that, though the person was destined to achieve something, she has done something to prevent this from occurring. Due to inertia or a lack of direction, a predestined event has not come into being. Alternatively, the subject has actively worked to ensure that a negative aspect has not come into being.

A line on the active but not the passive hand indicates an individual who has worked hard for the rewards in life. Variations in the lines between the two hands can also show a person who has learned from her mistakes. A person may have a line of escape (see page 75) on the passive but not on the active hand. This may indicate, for example, that the person has chosen to avoid alcohol, having learned a lesson from knowing an alcoholic.

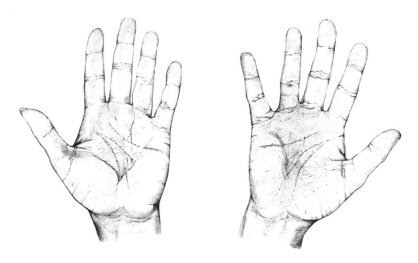

A line on the active hand but not on the passive hand shows a person who
has worked to achieve their rewards in life.

RISING AND FALLING LINES

When you are assessing a line, look out for little lines that cross, rise from, or lead down from it. These lines play a major role, regardless of how fine they are.

- Vertical lines rising from a line indicate that the subject has faced difficulties and has, through her own initiative, overcome any problems placed in the way.
- A line crossing right through another indicates a major hurdle. On the heart line it could indicate a competitor for a loved one's affection; on the head line, a rival for success at work. Tell your subject that being aware of these situations will help with overcoming them, as it is possible to succeed in virtually any situation with strength and purpose.
- Vertical lines heading downward from a line indicate a period when the subject has allowed a situation to get the better of her. You will often find lines of this type on the heart line. A break or an island may also accompany these lines, indicating that the situation was very upsetting. If you note lines of this type, emphasize the positive signs in the palm and note the subject's strengths so you can foster the self-esteem required for overcoming such difficulties in the future.

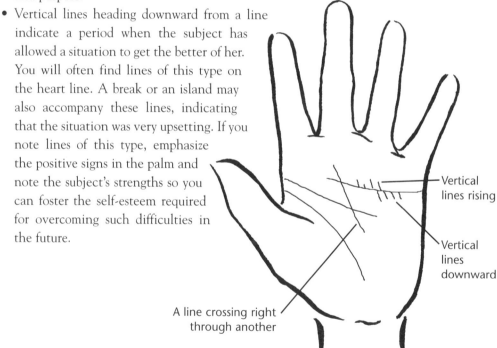

Vertical lines rising

Vertical lines downward

A line crossing right through another

THE LINE OF THE SUN

This is the sister line to the fate line and one of the lines on the hand most often not identified correctly. The line of the Sun, or the **Sun line**, is often confused with the **Mercury line**, or **health line**, which is unfortunate as these lines have very different meanings. If you look at this line in relation to another of its titles, the Apollo line, you will have a better chance of identifying it. The line of the Sun can arise from almost anywhere on the palm, but it ends very near to the ring, or Apollo, finger and is usually vertical.

The presence of the line of the Sun indicates that the person is due for outstanding success—as long as the fate line is strong. If the fate line is weak but there is a Sun line, then success could occur through luck rather than hard work. For example, this could be the hand of the person who is the millionth customer to walk into a shopping mall and be given a large prize.

As the line of the Sun rises to the **Apollo finger**, it is a good idea to examine this finger closely to see how well the subject will put her abilities to the test. A strong Sun line combined with a short, thin Apollo finger (see pages 119–120) suggests a person who will let opportunities pass by. However, when someone has a strong Apollo finger, expect nothing to stand between that person and success.

People with a line of the Sun on the palm often have a powerful ability to communicate their ideas. They are creative and innovative, and always put their thoughts into actions. People with this line are sensitive and strongly desire the fame that they have the potential to achieve. From a very early age they will set themselves on the path to

Line of
the Sun

riches and other rewards. One of the reasons for the success of those possessing this line is the tact and diplomacy they often possess. They will be able to assess a situation and manipulate it to their own benefit without upsetting anyone else.

The lack of a Sun line is not a negative trait—plenty of successful people do not have one. Often, those without a Sun line will achieve success in their chosen field, but they may not get the public acclaim that usually accompanies success.

SPECIAL FEATURES OF THE SUN LINE

- A person whose Sun line is linked by another line to the fate line will achieve success through working from home.
- This line definitely indicates success, but the origin of the success is probably to be found from the information revealed in the head line (whether it's through academic, creative, or other means). Some palmists tend to believe that this line indicates success or fame in the arts, but it could well be that the person will attain success in a business venture or may become a famous inventor. The answer is in the hand shape and the formation of the major lines on the hand.
- When the Sun line arises from the life line, expect great success at a time determined by the point where the Sun line leaves the life line.
- If the Sun line begins at the head line, success will come later in life and will be the result of the person's intellect.
- When the Sun line arises from the heart line, you can expect the owner of the hand to have an appreciation for a subject rather than a specific talent—this person would be a theater critic rather than a thespian, for example.
- A person with a number of lines arising from the Sun line is likely to have an abundance of ideas, but not necessarily the means to put them into action. Unfinished projects will probably litter this person's life.
- Having more than one Sun line indicates a multitalented person with an ability to shine in a variety of tasks.

THE MOUNTS AND THE SUN LINE

- A person with a Sun line arising from the mount of Neptune is likely to have special skills at dealing with people. Such a person could achieve success as a motivational speaker or life coach.
- A Sun line that arises in the outer mount of Mars is usually the mark of a person who will achieve success in politics or through community service.
- Should the Sun line arise from the mount of Luna, any success will come about with the help of others. It will result from teamwork rather than from the lone perseverance of one individual. A person with this marking who wants to succeed will have to make an effort to surround herself with the kind of people who will benefit her in this way.

MARKINGS ON THE SUN LINE

- An island indicates that there will be a period of scandal or disrepute, but as long as the island is not at the end of a line you can be confident that this will blow over.
- A Sun line that starts with a fork indicates a person with more than one talent, especially when this line arises in the mount of Mars.
- A person whose Sun line ends in a star is marked for extraordinary success and possibly worldwide fame. When the line is long, strong, and ends under the Apollo finger, it is likely that the person is an actor, artist, or musician destined for success in a creative field.
- A square on the line of the Sun is a positive omen. It indicates protection against the enemies one accumulates when in the public eye.

THE HEALTH LINE

The health, or Mercury, line is often confused with the line of the Sun, as their positions on the palm are similar. The health line can start somewhere near the life line, but unlike the Sun line it ends somewhere underneath the little, or Mercury, finger, rather than the ring finger. However, while the appearance of a Sun line on a palm is a positive trait, the health line can indicate health problems and is considered a more negative line. That said, there are many positive aspects regarding the presence of a health line on the hand—it just depends on what other signs accompany it.

Health line

MORE THAN JUST HEALTH

When this line is present on a hand, it can indicate problems with health. Some kind of physical weakness is suggested when the line is fragmented or poorly drawn. However, the presence of the Mercury line also indicates a great communicator. When assessing this line, you should also look at the **Mercury finger**. If the person has a weak, thin, or short Mercury finger, her efforts to communicate will often be thwarted. However, if the Mercury finger is strong, then you can expect the subject to be a great orator, successful at communicating her ideas to society at large or to others on an individual basis.

On a hand with other positive indications, a long, strong health line can be a sign that the person is destined for success with money. On a square palm with a good head line, for example, it would be clear that the person with a strong health line will build a successful business and accumulate a great deal of money as a result.

A straight, clear health line that runs across the palm with no breaks indicates a lively, energetic individual who will often make her living through the gift of the gab. Those who work in public relations, where their success lies in their ability to charm their audience and talk up a subject, will often have a strong health line.

Any person who has this line is bound to be conscious of health and this can manifest itself in a positive or negative manner: the person will either follow a healthy regime of diet and exercise or will worry about her health and go to various extremes, such as swinging from a strict diet to binge eating.

If the health line is thin and wavers across the palm, health problems and a nervous disposition are indicated. People with these lines often tend toward hypochondria and may be susceptible to psychosomatic illness.

A thin, pale health line can also indicate problems with the stomach and the liver, and if these issues are not solved early, they can lead to more serious problems.

MARKINGS ON THE HEALTH LINE

- A **cross** on the health line is a warning of potential accidents. The subject needs to be extremely cautious in any dangerous situations.
- A square on the health line means that the person will be protected, either by medical intervention in the case of an illness or through the help of business associates.
- An island on the health line indicates an illness that will result in hospitalization.
- A health line with many breaks reveals stumbling blocks in communication. The subject may know what she wants to say, but not how to say it.

MARRIAGE LINES

The **marriage lines**, or relationship lines, are horizontal lines that can be found above the heart line underneath the little, or Mercury, finger on the outside of the palm. They can be fine or quite deeply etched, depending on the type of hand they appear on and the nature of the relationships they show. For example, on a psychic hand with delicate lines the marriage lines would also be quite fine, regardless of the importance of the relationship.

While these are traditionally called marriage lines, relationship lines might be a more appropriate term, as these lines indicate relationships of significance, not just marriages. It is therefore possible for a person to have a number of these lines on the palm, and the lines can come and go depending on the significance of that relationship at the current time. Interestingly, while the majority of women will have these lines on their palms, not all men will, even if they are married or involved in a major relationship.

It is not only relationships of a sexual nature that show up on the palm. You may have a soul mate in life and not have a sexual relationship with this person, and yet, because of the importance of this person to your life, she will be etched into the palm. A long, solid line reveals a happy, stable relationship of great significance to that person's life. If a line is weak or short, you can expect the relationship to be of a similar nature.

Children lines

Marriage lines

Forks at the end of a line can mean a split, while a line that is made up of breaks indicates an on-again, off-again relationship.

It is important to emphasize the point that we have the ability to change the lines on our hands through our behavior. Hence, a relationship line that appears to come to a premature end can be repaired with hard work or counseling, if both parties so desire.

TIMING

To set a time frame for the relationships indicated by these lines, divide the section of the palm from the heart line up to the base of the Mercury finger into three—birth to mid-twenties, mid-twenties to fifties, and fifties and beyond. Only significant relationships show up in these lines—if a person has had many sexual partners, and these partners played small roles in her emotional life, you would not expect them to show up here.

CHILDREN LINES

These lines are often so fine that viewing them with the naked eye is near impossible and a magnifying glass and strong light are often necessary to make a proper identification. **Children lines** arise from the marriage line and appear as fine, vertical markings. Strictly speaking, each line indicates one child, but you must bear in mind that not only live-born children appear on a palm. Miscarriages, stillbirths, and abortions can all appear, and this is why it is important to realize that children lines indicate potential only.

Some palmists believe that longer lines indicate boys, while the shorter lines reveal girls. Considering that the lines themselves are often difficult to identify, it would be extremely hard to try to guess at gender!

A line that splits in two reveals twins; if it splits in three, triplets are expected.

If a large number of children is indicated on a palm, this may mean that the person has the capacity for caring for a lot of children, rather than parenting them all. She may be a teacher, a doctor, or a counselor, or may foster a number of children over the years. Fostered, adopted, and stepchildren are also often marked. The children lines indicate the space in a person's heart to love and care for a child, not that person's reproductive capabilities.

RASCETTES

The **rascettes**, or **bracelets**, are found below the palm, encircling the palm side of the wrist. They are considered a fortunate marking and are usually found in groups of three or more. In ancient palmistry tradition, it is said that you can expect thirty years of luck for each rascette. When gauging the rascettes, the one furthest from the palm is considered the first thirty years and so on, up to the top.

Some palmists also believe that each bracelet is an indication of the length of our lives. With this method you need to allocate twenty-five years of life to each bracelet. However, this method is very unreliable and should not be used to indicate length of life, as some people have no rascettes, while others may only have one or two.

If the bracelet is halved or broken, then the luck will run out before its time. But if more bracelets are present, do not fret—more luck is on its way!

A person who has three rascettes that are all clear, strong, and fully formed can expect great fortune throughout life. Things will come easily to this person.

When the final bracelet curves in the middle and enters the palm, this indicates gynecological problems for women, particularly in the middle years.

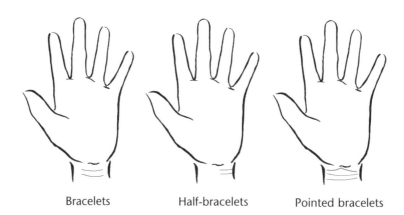

Bracelets   Half-bracelets   Pointed bracelets

TRAVEL LINES

Some people have a large number of lines entering the palm from the mount of Luna. These are travel lines. In order to understand their precise meaning, you really need to read and understand the rest of the palm. For example, in a palm that indicates a cautious and conservative person, a long travel line does not point to a long trip overseas—it could merely indicate an annual vacation in a coastal town close to home.

The term "travel line" may be a bit of a misnomer, as it is not only travel that is indicated in these lines. Restlessness is the primary feature revealed by travel lines, and it is possible that someone with a number of these lines will never even leave the living room. That said, this kind of person is bound to have an interest in other places and cultures. This person could be immersed in studies of Egyptian culture with no desire to view the Sphinx up close. Or the home may be decorated in a Mexican or Japanese style even though the owner has never been to either country.

The real traveler has an adventurous palm and many journeys are often mapped out on this hand. Short, pale lines usually indicate short journeys, while longer and deeper lines indicate extensive trips overseas.

If a businessperson travels a lot for work reasons, most of these trips will not have an impact on the palm, but an around-the-world trip for pleasure will. It is the importance of the travel to the person's life that is revealed on the palm, rather than the travel itself.

People with a travel line crossing the line of fate may find that a vacation changes their lives. They may meet the love of their life abroad or they could discover a passion that becomes their life's mission.

GIRDLE OF VENUS

The **girdle of Venus** is a half-circle at the top of the palm between the **Jupiter finger** and the Mercury finger. It can be complete or broken, finely etched or deeply marked, chained, frayed, or tessellated. It indicates sensitivity, particularly in relation to the feelings of others.

If this line is straight, strong, and clear, it indicates a person in emotional turmoil. This person may seem outwardly happy and extroverted and be a good communicator, but her behavior may be extreme. People with this line can be excessively flirtatious and subject to extremes of emotion: dizzy highs may be juxtaposed with deep lows.

When the girdle of Venus is made up of small fragments, it indicates a much more temperate outlook. People with this type of line may still crave excitement, but life will be much more straightforward for them than for the person with the straight, clear girdle of Venus described above.

When both the girdle of Venus and the line of escape (see page 75) appear on the palm—a rare occurrence—this could mean that the person is seriously tempted to overindulge, particularly in sensual acts such as sex and eating.

LINE OF INTUITION

If you notice a long half-circle linking the mount of Luna and the mount of Mercury on a palm, you are reading the palm of a person with exceptional intuition. People with this marking, called the **line of intuition**, can understand others within an instant of meeting, and their bright, sensitive minds make them ideal psychics.

Often, people with this line will use their talents in their careers. For example, their great understanding of others makes them successful as counselors, healers, or writers. Sometimes, though, those with the line of intuition can be overly sensitive and easily hurt by the criticism of those around them.

People who have a broken line of intuition on the palm are best advised to limit their forays into the psychic world, as their health could be affected. They may have a tendency to overempathize and may take other people's problems to heart. If this is the case, such people would benefit from meditation and should avoid violent or disturbing television or films wherever possible, as these could affect their well-being and mental health.

The lack of a line of intuition does not indicate an absence of intuition and often there are other signs on the palm that reveal a subject's insight into the lives of others. Some hand types, such as the psychic-handed person, do not need to have this line as an indication of intuition. The hand shape itself reveals their ability. But if they do have this line, along with other signs, their power can be great and could be a major force in their lives.

MONEY LINES

There are several **money lines** that indicate whether a person is likely to inherit money or earn a substantial salary. As what is considered substantial to one person may be just a small bonus to another, this is another area in which you need to use caution when reading.

- If you find a line that runs straight up from the base of the palm and ends under the Jupiter finger in a star, you can be certain that you have found a natural moneymaker. Everything this person touches will turn to gold.

- If you see a small, partly curved line between the Saturn (middle) finger and the Apollo (ring) finger, with the line curving toward the Apollo finger, this may mean that the person is likely to inherit money.

- A **triangle** on the inside of the life line indicates that a person will come into money easily, but not by inheritance or through earnings. Winning money would be the most likely way. You can normally predict the period of time in which this will occur, but it is important to warn your subject not to spend too much on anticipating this win, so that the benefits are not outweighed by the outlay. The triangle marking indicates, instead, that this will be easy money, gained from simply buying a lottery ticket on a whim, rather than from diligently trying to win by buying a ticket every week.

THE LINE OF ESCAPE

The line of escape, or the poison or **allergy line**, runs straight across the mount of Luna low on the palm toward the life line, and if this line appears it is a major warning of an extreme sensitivity to certain substances. It may therefore be evident on the palms of people who have a tendency to alcoholism, drug addiction, and other addictive behaviors. The line may only appear on one hand, but regardless of whether it is on the active or passive hand there is still a need for caution and restraint.

People with this line can often be highly allergic—those with potentially fatal anaphylactic reactions can have this line. The name is indicative of how people with this line react to substances to which they are sensitive. If a baby or child has this line, extreme caution needs to be exercised when introducing potentially allergenic foods, particularly nuts and wheat. The later these are introduced into the diet, the better.

Line of escape

THE MYSTIC CROSS

The **mystic cross** appears as an X between the head and the heart line and indicates an interest in the occult. It does not necessarily indicate talent in the area, just that the person finds the subject intriguing. A person with this marking will often have a large library containing books on a variety of esoteric subjects. This person will know the basics of tarot, will have practiced feng shui in the home, and will have dedicated some of the garden to "magical" herbs. But not everyone who is interested in the occult has this marking, and it can fade and reappear at different stages of life as interests wax and wane.

75

THE LUCKY M

The **lucky M** is the formation of the four major lines—life, heart, head, and fate—into an M. Traditionally, this marking, when found on a woman's hand, showed that she was destined for a successful marriage, whereas on a man's hand it meant success with money. Now that we are living in times that are a little more enlightened, this line could be interpreted to mean success in both areas for men and women—a happy love life and more than enough money to live comfortably.

It is important to note that, as the fate line can appear later in life, it is possible for a person to not have this formation at first, but for the lucky M to appear as the fate line lengthens. That said, not everyone with all four lines will have this marking, which is why it is worthy of comment if it does appear.

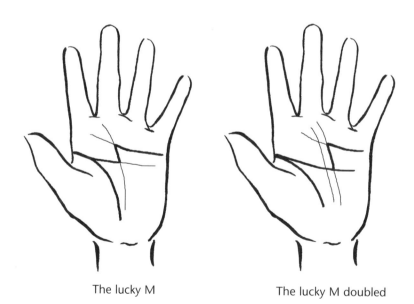

The lucky M   The lucky M doubled

OTHER MARKINGS

- Stars are four or five lines that cross over each other to form a star shape, and normally indicate success.

- Triangles are most fortuitous when they appear and indicate success. They show that the subject has a powerful brain and is able to sum up situations very quickly. Triangles on a mount (see Chapter Five) enhance the qualities of that mount.

- Perfect circles are very rare. What at first appears to be a circle is more likely to be an oval-shaped island. When a circle is found on the **mount of Apollo** (see page 92), great success is assured.

- **Worry lines** are a lot of fine lines on the surface of the palm that show nervous tension. People with a series of lines running across the mount of Venus from the base of the thumb have let their worries get the better of them. Should one of these lines cross the life line, then these worries have affected their health or will do so in the future.

- The **family ring** is a chain that runs around the base of the thumb. Oddly enough, the more chained, the better with this marking. It indicates the subject's relationship with family. The deeper and more chained the markings, the closer the family. A ring that straightens up or becomes finer at some point shows a growing away from the family.

REVIEW

There are an enormous variety of secondary lines that can appear on a person's palm and it is in these lines that we can ascertain any special talents or interests. It is important to note that, while certain lines and markings indicate success or talent in a particular area, not every person with that talent will have the marking. It is also interesting how these lines and markings can appear and vanish overnight depending on a person's interests and awareness.

While some lines are considered positive and others negative, we can find some positive messages even in a negative marking. This is why it is particularly worthwhile for parents to examine the palms of their children, not only to gain insight into their character but also to reveal areas of weakness that can be strengthened over time. For example, a child with a line of escape would need educating from a very early age about the dangers of drugs, particularly with the parents leading by example. A child with worry lines can be taught stress-relieving exercises in order to overcome her anxieties.

In regards to luck, it is worthwhile to remember that the best thing about luck is that it can be made. Whether you have good luck or bad luck really depends on your outlook. It really is a good idea to figure out whether you are an optimist or a pessimist, whether you view the glass as half-full or half-empty. If you're a half-empty kind of individual, you may be surprised at how shifting your perspective can radically alter the direction of your life.

Remember that it is the sunny, confident individuals who believe that they deserve good fortune to come their way who actually experience good fortune, not the miserable pessimists who just "know" that only bad things ever happen to them.

WORKBOOK EXERCISES

1. In your journal, trace the outline of your hand and mark out the secondary lines, according to the descriptions in this chapter.
2. Put the diagram aside for a day and then come back and try to identify the markings without glancing back at the explanations in the chapter. How many could you identify correctly?
3. Next, write down your own explanation of what these lines and markings mean.
   • What does this line represent for me?
   • What are three aspirations you hold for each line? (For example, for the health line: "I want to quit smoking.")
4. How many secondary lines do you have on your hands? List them. Then list the secondary lines that appear on your copies of the palms of friends and family members.
5. When a marking signifies ill health or worries, what advice would you give your subject? For example, if your subject had the Mercury line and a line of escape, what lifestyle changes would you recommend? (It is important to realize that the palmist is not a medical practitioner. If you need to point out the potential problems of any substances liable to cause addictions, leave it up to the person to take that advice.)
6. What other markings would you look to for help? Would you consider the life line relevant in this situation? What about the head line and heart line?
7. In difficult situations, do you have a tendency to view the glass as half-full or half-empty?
8. To maintain a positive outlook, start every day by meditating, just for one minute, on one good thing about yourself. Positively affirm this thought throughout the day. If you constantly tell yourself, "I'm a good person who deserves to have good things happen to me," then it is more likely they will. Expect luck to come your way—and who knows, maybe it will.

CHAPTER FIVE

THE MOUNTS

Learn about the mounts of the hand, their significance, and how they affect a reading.

Mounts are present in various guises on all hands and reveal talents, tastes, and tendencies. The history of the names of the mounts can be traced back to the Roman gods and goddesses and the planets named after them. It is fascinating how these mounts take on the traits attributed to these deities and planets (see Chapter One). These traits are embedded in our language. Take the word "saturnine," for example. It means gloomy and sluggish, behaviors attributed to those born under the influence of Saturn. So pay particular attention when one mount or finger dominates the rest.

The mounts are an ideal place to start when reading the palm of a child, as they give a strong indication of interests and talents. However, like the lines on the hand, the mounts are inclined to change as the person's outlook changes. A person with an underdeveloped mount can, with encouragement and direction, change an attitude and increase the size of the mount accordingly.

Mount of Saturn

Mount of Apollo

Mount of Jupiter

Inner mount of Mars

Mount of Mercury

Mount of Venus

Outer mount of Mars

Mount of Luna

Mount of Neptune

EXAMINING THE MOUNTS

When you are making your first assessment of a person's palm, before even attempting a reading you should be on particular alert for anything that stands out on the palm. This is why the sense of touch is often as important as sight when reading a palm. You will need to press on the fleshy areas to see if they yield, and to turn over the palm and examine it from all angles in good light.

The best way to view the mounts is to hold the palm flat, directly in front of your eyes, so that you are looking at it from the wrist to the fingertips. In this way you will be able to judge the positioning of the mounts and see if any mounts seem to be dominant. Closing your eyes and running your fingers over the palm's surface can sometimes give you a clearer "view" than the strongest of visual examinations. Be prepared to experiment and be tactile. Palmistry is an art in which touch is vital—and being in close contact with another's skin will also help increase your clairvoyant abilities. Whenever you are unable to see something, try to feel it. It gives a whole new perspective on the matter.

Some palms are very fleshy, with high mounts, while the occasional palm is flat. Still others have indentations or even huge swellings. It is this myriad of possible combinations that makes palmistry such a fascinating craft.

DEGREES OF DEVELOPMENT

The lack of a mount is just as significant as the presence of a mount: whatever the presence of a mount reveals, its absence indicates the opposite. So while a well-developed mount of Venus indicates a passionate individual, the lack of this mount would indicate an individual who rarely feels strongly about anything—including sex.

When assessing a mount, you will need to determine if it is well developed, overdeveloped, or underdeveloped. It may be difficult for you to recognize these traits at first, but after you have examined a few palms you will be surprised at how clearly some mounts stand out. With practice, you will readily be able to assess a strong mount and a weak mount—both types really do stand out. You do not really need to take into consideration the feature's size. What is worthy of comment is whether it appears much larger than another of its kind.

The ideal mount is well developed, firm to the touch, and not too fleshy. For example, an underdeveloped mount of Luna indicates a lack of imagination and creativity, so if you see this in a child you should limit television viewing, increase exposure to art and poetry, and ensure that crayons, paper, and pens are always available to help swell the child's creative tide.

THE ASSOCIATED FINGERS

When assessing the mounts that fall under the fingers, you should take care to assess the relevant finger at the same time to help confirm any opinion. For example, a strong mount accompanied by a weak finger has a completely different meaning than a strong finger and an overdeveloped mount. If both mount and finger are strong and overdeveloped, any traits will be amplified. For example, a strong mount of Mercury combined with a long Mercury finger would indicate that this person was inordinately blessed with powerful skills of communication. Alternatively, if a weak mount or finger is accompanied by a strong finger or mount, the positive attributes are diluted—perhaps the person tends to doubt his abilities.

THE HOLLOW PALM

Beliefs about the **hollow palm** are based in antiquity. Superstition held that if you had a hollow palm you were likely to come into money and be able to hold onto it. That said, most palms have a hollow in the center due to the height of the mounts around them. The flat area in the center is also known as the **plain of Mars**, and it is in this area where the **battle cross** can be found. In ancient times, having the marking of a battle cross on one's palm was an indication of a noble death in battle, but now it usually indicates a person who is extremely passionate about a specific cause.

Ideally, the center of the palm should be flat rather than indented. A flat palm indicates a person with a good balance of caution and inquisitiveness. When the center of the palm is deeply inverted, the subject is likely to be overly cautious and fearful of change.

You should also pay heed to any lines or markings that appear on the mounts. If a line ends on a mount, it takes on the aspects of that mount.

WORKBOOK EXERCISES

We all have something we're fearful of: rejection, ridicule, public speaking. You have three options when it comes to fear: you can reject it, nurture it, or embrace it. Write down three of your prominent fears and how you might take steps to overcome these.

MARKINGS ON THE MOUNTS

 A grille may appear on any of the mounts, with the following meanings:

 • On Mercury: A person who is not afraid to lie in order to get his own way.

 • On Apollo: Someone so hungry for fame that the preoccupation with vanity will often drive others away.

 • On Saturn: A perpetually gloomy person who views everything negatively.

 • On Jupiter: An innately selfish personality.

 • On Venus: Someone incapable of controlling passionate urges.

 • On Luna: Someone almost impossible to please.

The size of the mount on which the grille lies is also important—when the mount is large, the qualities will be emphasized; they will be lessened if the mount is small or indented.

 Stars (see page 77) indicate success. To find out where the success lies, look to the mount on which the star lies. For example, a star on the mount of Mercury could indicate success as a public speaker.

MOUNT OF LUNA

The mount of Luna is found on the bottom outer edge of the palm, and heads up toward the little finger. It is normally the next largest mount on the palm after the mount of Venus and is the area where creativity and imagination flow.

The ideal mount of Luna should be broad and well shaped, with a slightly rounded look. People who have the mount of Luna as the dominant mount on their hands will have a tendency to spend their time daydreaming rather than working. Every aspect of their lives will be subject to flights of fantasy.

An overdeveloped mount of Luna can reveal realism suffering at the hands of creativity, or a person with original ideas often able to convince others of his brilliance, but with nothing ever coming to fruition. Such a person, whose whole life is subject to fantasy and whose expectations exceed reality, may have difficulty coping in the real world.

A person with a well-developed mount of Luna would have a strong love for family and home, an active imagination, and a marked romantic streak. People involved in the creative arts and literature normally have this feature of the palm firm and well developed. Sensitivity and spirituality are also revealed by a well-developed mount of Luna. People with this feature are often humanitarians, keenly interested in the welfare of others. They also tend to be involved in religion, with a positive community attitude.

People with underdeveloped mounts, however, can be selfish. It is not that they deliberately ignore others, rather that they do not give them a second thought. An underdeveloped mount of Luna can indicate a person who is realistic to the point of being unimaginative and dull. Such a person would be happy to work under others, but incapable of finding innovative solutions. Progress at work may be slow, with more creative colleagues gaining the promotions and awards.

CROSSING LINES

If the head line ends on the mount of Luna, the person will undoubtedly be creative at work, with an imagination that produces innovative ideas. Such a person is destined for career success. A unique individual will have a line of success that starts on the mount of Luna. In this case only such an extraordinary person could capitalize on a very unusual opportunity that requires both boldness and creativity to succeed.

 WORKBOOK EXERCISES

If you have an under- or overdeveloped mount of Luna, you should practice the following to balance this feature.

1. For an overdeveloped mount of Luna, spend a few minutes per day reflecting on the following: "Order and structure help define my creativity."
2. For an underdeveloped mount of Luna, spend a few minutes per day reflecting on the following: "I allow my imagination to burst free when I recall the child within."
3. Define five goals that you wish to achieve within the next five years. What steps do you need to take to ensure success? What can you do each day to encourage positive attributes to balance your current qualities?

MOUNT OF VENUS

As Venus is the goddess of love, it is easy to remember the theme to which this mount relates. It indicates passion and the way we live our lives. The mount of Venus is the third **phalange** of the thumb and is identifiable as the fleshy area at the base of the thumb that is encircled by the life line. A well-developed mount will cover about a third of the palm and will be nicely rounded and firm. A mount like this will reveal a person with a zest for life, passionate about everything—and with a satisfying love life.

DEGREES OF DEVELOPMENT

An overdeveloped mount means sensuality has run amok. An excessive love for sex, food, or drink will rule the subject's life. If the overdeveloped mount is also hard, aggression could be present. A red mount of this type indicates that this aggression may be manifest in sexual relationships. Sex may be an animalistic need for this individual rather than an act of love.

An underdeveloped mount shows a person lacking in intensity. Such a person will plod through life without much interest. If the mount is underdeveloped because the life line closely hugs the thumb, then it is a fearful nature that is holding this person back. Sex will take a back seat when the mount of Venus is underdeveloped; if the partner also has a small mount of Venus, no problems may arise. However, it is a good idea for couples to compare each other's mounts of Venus to see how sexually compatible they are, otherwise one partner may believe the pair is sexually intimate "all the time" while the other believes the opposite.

The mount of Venus also reveals how we relate to others. Those with a well-developed mount tend to have good relationships with family, friends, and coworkers, while an underdeveloped mount could indicate a loner with poor relationships with others.

That said, this is one of the easiest mounts to alter. Simply falling in love or stepping up sexual intimacy can increase the size of this mount rather quickly. Happiness in love can bring happiness in many other areas of life as well.

 WORKBOOK EXERCISES

If you have an underdeveloped or overdeveloped mount of Venus, you should practice the following.

1. For an overdeveloped mount of Venus, spend a few minutes per day reflecting on the following: "I am satisfied with just a small taste of what I desire."

2. For an underdeveloped mount of Venus, spend a few minutes per day reflecting on the following: "I am a sensuous individual who deserves to be rewarded."

3. An imbalance in the mount of Venus can often be a result of a poorly defined self-image and ego. It's important to acknowledge that we deserve the best in life. Make a vow to yourself to only accept the best—because you are the best. Do the best possible job you can, be the best possible partner in your relationship, be the best child, the best parent—once you are the best you can possibly be, you will only accept the same from others. You'll be surprised at how many people will naturally fall into step with your expectations. But don't allow the behavior of others to influence yours—be the best person only to please yourself, not to live up to another person's expectations. Write down five things you would like to do better in your life. Next to each of these, write down three ways you will go about achieving it.

THE INNER MOUNT OF MARS

Mars is the god of war, but that does not mean that the **mount of Mars** indicates only aggression or a battle. There are two mounts of Mars—**inner** and **outer**—otherwise known as the positive and negative mounts. Their names are based on the plain of the hand on which they rest.

The inner mount of Mars is a small mount that lies above the mount of Venus, between the thumb and the index finger. This mount is indicative of physical strength and the ability to persevere. When this mount is well developed, it indicates courage and the strength to overcome obstacles and challenges. When a strong mount of Venus accompanies a strong Mars positive, there can be a tendency to aggression. It can signal the tendency to react immediately and negatively to any sign of criticism and to throw temper tantrums rather than constructively seeking a solution if a task is hard to complete.

A weak inner mount of Mars is the sign of a very passive individual, the kind of person who can easily be manipulated. This person will have little sense of self and will be afraid of challenging others. A weak inner mount, however, can also be the sign of a bully—someone with so little self-esteem that ridiculing others is his sole form of satisfaction.

THE OUTER MOUNT OF MARS

This mount is found just below the mount of Mercury, usually between the heart line and the head line. Just as the inner mount of Mars stands for physical courage, the outer mount of Mars stands for mental courage. This mount symbolizes determination.

A well-formed outer mount of Mars reflects a person who can resist manipulation by others and has the tenacity to stay on his chosen path. A firm mount of Mars negative that is enclosed by the heart line and the head line indicates someone who is rational and able to use common sense to make the most of any situation.

This mount also reveals a person's moral convictions. If it is underdeveloped, expect the sense of morality to be weak; if overdeveloped, it may signal a moralistic zealot. An overdeveloped mount of Mars negative indicates that violence can occur; people of this type may use force when standing up for their rights.

When the mount is small or soft, it reveals a person who is easily dominated. People with this marking may lack a sense of self and often act for the benefit of others rather than themselves. They will never speak up to state their social or other preferences. They are also likely to get overlooked at work, as they are disinclined to speak up and ask for a raise or a promotion.

 ## WORKBOOK EXERCISES

So often we are caught up in how others perceive us that we don't really know who we are. We can spend so much time trying to say the right thing or wear the right clothes that we are not clear as to what our own values and tastes are. Just like Mars, our lives are about balance and it is important to maintain this balance. Here are some ways you can bring balance to your life:

1. Write down your five greatest strengths and your five greatest weaknesses.
2. Compose a strategy to overcome your weaknesses and turn them to your advantage.
3. Each day when you awaken, state your top five strengths as an affirmation.
4. Compose an affirmation to overcome any negative aspects of your life, for example: "I am calm in the face of adversity. I stop, take a deep breath, and count to ten before responding in a calm, intelligent manner."

MOUNT OF JUPITER

The mount of Jupiter falls under the finger of Jupiter, or the index finger, and its traits are spirituality, self-confidence, charisma, and inspiration. Ideally, this mount should rest directly under the index finger. If it veers off toward the edge of the palm, it can signify self-obsession. If it leans toward the Saturn (middle) finger, the person will tend toward introversion.

When this mount is well developed, the person will have a firm sense of self and, because of his strong sense of self-esteem, will prove an inspiration and a leader to others. An underdeveloped mount reveals a person filled with insecurity and lacking ambition or any interest in life.

When Jupiter is the dominant mount, rather than in balance with the other mounts, the positive traits can be magnified to such a degree that they become excessive. They may manifest as self-absorption and a tendency to be overconfident in one's own abilities. An overdeveloped mount of Jupiter is often the sign of an egoist who tends to be overbearing. Alternatively, it could be the sign of a person obsessed with spirituality to the point of becoming involved in a dangerous cult.

The **teacher's square** is a square-shaped marking found on the mount of Jupiter, the sign of a person who is gifted with the ability to teach others.

WORKBOOK EXERCISES

1. How do you express your spirituality? Name three other ways you could enjoy doing this.
2. Consider these words: "Jupiter is the planet that gives us our desire to succeed—the need to excel at everything we do." List five areas in which you want to succeed.

MOUNT OF SATURN

Saturn is associated with legal matters, and this mount therefore represents introspection and the quest for truth and balance. Life is complex and we often have to sit back, reflect, and sift through all the contradictory experiences and information we encounter. Saturn helps us do this.

The mount of Saturn helps reduce the effects of the more dramatic mounts, such as Jupiter. It is located under the middle, or Saturn, finger and is rarely seen in a well-developed state. Generally this mount seems quite flat and may appear to drift toward one of the other fingers. A normally developed mount of Saturn reveals a well-balanced individual who is able to enjoy the time he spends alone, reveling in moments of solitude. Study is favored when this mount is well developed, as are emotional balance and fidelity.

Conversely, if this mount is overdeveloped, all of these traits become negative and the person will be a loner, not knowing how to enjoy time spent in the company of others. Such a person will also be introspective to the point of being unable to do anything without endlessly rationalizing it.

An underdeveloped mount of Saturn, or a void, indicates a person who has no ability to socialize, because he has no sense of humor and is often irresponsible.

WORKBOOK EXERCISES

1. Would you say your life is more work or more play? List five things you could do to better balance these elements in your life.
2. Write down three goals you have in life. On a scale of one to ten (with ten being most), how much do you want to achieve these goals? List five steps you can take toward achieving them.

MOUNT OF APOLLO

The mount of Apollo is found under the ring, or Apollo, finger. This mount reveals a talent in the arts and a love of beauty. Apollo is the god of power and self-expression, hence the affinity with creativity.

When this mount is well developed, the person will probably have strong aesthetic sensibilities: a great love of beauty and an appreciation for music and art. Often, people with this marking are themselves talented in the arts and have no problems applying these talents to becoming successful.

That said, such a person does not have to be an "artist" in the literal sense of the word. Those with a well-developed mount of Apollo will often have a beautifully decorated home or a garden filled with perfumed delights, and may always be beautifully dressed.

When the mount is overdeveloped, money or fame will often take precedence over creativity, and artistic integrity will readily be compromised for a healthy paycheck. People with this marking are so obsessed with beauty that they may go to extremes, using plastic surgery and excessive dieting to achieve their ideals.

An underdeveloped mount of Apollo signals a person to whom aesthetics mean nothing. Such a person will live in a functional, undecorated home, eat meals designed purely to satisfy caloric needs, and find no time for reading or listening to music for pleasure's sake.

WORKBOOK EXERCISES

1. Consider these words: "Apollo gives us our purpose in life and sheds light on the path we are to take to achieve success. Apollo also represents immediacy—the fact that if we are going to do something, then we should do it now." Name one thing that you should be doing that you are not. What can you do today to help achieve this?

MOUNT OF MERCURY

The mount of Mercury is where success in business is often shown. Located under the Mercury, or little, finger, the mount of Mercury, just like the god, rules communication. Pay particular attention to the Mercury finger if it is long (see pages 121–122), as this indicates extraordinary talent in this area.

A well-developed mount of Mercury is found on people with excellent communication skills, those able to get their ideas across verbally. They will know what they want in life and how to achieve their goals. People with this feature will often make successful careers out of speaking, becoming public speakers, radio announcers, salespeople, or diplomats. They will be sociable, friendly, and intelligent, easy to get along with, and likely to succeed in all areas of life.

There is no real negative aspect to an overdeveloped mount of Mercury, although it can be a little difficult to keep people with this feature quiet. The sound of silence may often seem too alien for them, so they will chatter on without really thinking about what they are saying.

An underdeveloped mount of Mercury is the mark of a poor communicator—a person who knows what to say but not how to put it across. This is particularly so in personal relationships, where someone with this feature will find it difficult to express his needs to a partner and discussion will often degenerate into arguments or tears.

WORKBOOK EXERCISES

1. Consider these words: "Mercury's role is to help us become effective communicators. Often, we will find that we are so focused on others, particularly on what they may think of us, that we lose our ability to communicate effectively." Is there something that you have been reluctant to communicate to someone? Why? What would you like to say?

MOUNT OF NEPTUNE

At the base of the wrist, between the mounts of Luna and Venus, lies the mount of Neptune. As it joins the two mounts that represent, respectively, imagination and the conscious enjoyment of life, it is considered that the mount of Neptune represents the link between the conscious and the subconscious. People who have this mount well developed will revel in their ability to speak in public. They will often be well-balanced individuals with sharp minds and quick wits.

The planet Neptune rules dreams and illusions. Neptune is a type of muse and helps draw out each individual's creative talents.

MEDITATION ON NEPTUNE

If your mount of Neptune is out of balance (either underdeveloped or overdeveloped), practice the following meditations to help bring your creativity to the fore.

On a waning moon: Sit comfortably outdoors, allowing yourself to come in contact with the earth. Think about the immediate area that surrounds you, then start to consider yourself as part of your street, your town, your country. Picture yourself and the place you take on the earth as important, with a valuable role in your society. Allow any negative thoughts and energies to flow through your body and out the top of your head.

On a waxing moon: Sit comfortably outdoors, allowing yourself to come in contact with the earth. Focus on the planet Neptune and on the creativity that resides there. Slowly allow this creativity to enter your body and manifest itself in whatever way you desire.

One night each week, dedicate yourself to creative pursuits. Light a white candle and work uninterrupted for at least one hour. Remember that you are a creative being who adds a little bit of beauty to this world—enjoy.

THE HEALTH MOUNT

Strictly speaking, this is not really a mount. However, the **health mount** is a good indicator of the subject's physical constitution. It appears when the hand is made into a fist, with the thumb tightly curled up. The mound that appears on the back of the hand, between the thumb and the index finger, looks like a mouse and is the health mount.

A firm mount shows a strong, healthy person with good resistance to disease. This person will rarely fall ill and any illness will seldom last long. A flabby or weak mount indicates a person with a poor constitution who is always suffering from one sickness or another. It is interesting to note how quickly this mount can change. If a normally healthy person is in the throes of a severe illness, the usually firm mount may become flabby and may almost disappear. Then, when good health returns, so will the firm mount.

 WORKBOOK EXERCISES

Our health is a reflection of the way in which we are taking care of our body. If we get sick it is often because we are not doing this adequately. Try the following:

1. Allow sufficient time for sleep—at least six hours, but preferably eight. Don't drink coffee or other beverages containing caffeine after 3 p.m. Allow yourself downtime an hour before you go to bed: have a bath, relax, and don't watch stimulating television.
2. Maintain a balanced diet as often as possible. Drink six to eight glasses of water a day. Eat plenty of fruit and vegetables each day and limit consumption of processed food.
3. Exercise for at least twenty minutes, three times a week. (Walking at the mall counts as exercise!)
4. Learn to say no. Often, stress arises because we take on too much. Learn to say "No, I won't be able to do that," and people will respect you and your stress levels will drop. Tackle tasks one step at a time—and don't move on to the next task until you've finished the first one.
5. Extremes of emotions can also wreak havoc on our well-being. Whenever possible, avoid situations that cause you undue emotional anxiety.

THE CREATIVE CURVE

Look at the outer side of the palm from the Mercury finger to the wrist. If the palm appears to curve, you have noted what is called the **creative curve**. The greater the curve, the greater the level of creativity.

Take note of where the curve originates and ends, as not all creative curves run the full length of the palm. A person with a curve that is short and starts at the top of the palm will find it difficult to put ideas into practice. A curve in the middle is ideal as this indicates a person who is creative and can turn ideas into reality. A curve at the base of the palm is the sign of a practical, realistic person.

REVIEW

The mounts are where the true secrets of the soul lie. Each mount corresponds to a planet or a Roman god or goddess. In order to gain a complete understanding of your subject, always check these raised areas on the palm. The first thing to note is which mount stands out from the others. A hand indicating balance has all of the mounts in a well-developed state, firm but not fleshy, and rounded but not voluptuous.

These are the attributes of a well-developed mount:
- **mount of Luna**: creativity, imagination, and family orientation
- **mount of Venus**: love, sex, and appetites
- **inner mount of Mars**: strength and stamina
- **outer mount of Mars**: morality and conviction
- **mount of Jupiter**: confidence, spirituality, and inspiration
- **mount of Saturn**: responsibility, duty, and seriousness
- **mount of Apollo**: aesthetic appreciation, artistic qualities, and talent
- **mount of Mercury**: business success and communication
- **mount of Neptune**: balance and quick-wittedness

WORKBOOK EXERCISES

1. Start by examining the nine mounts on your own hands. First look at the mounts on your passive hand and then compare them with those on your active hand. Be honest with yourself—try not to edit any "negative" qualities. Make notes about the following for both hands:
   - Do any of the mounts stand out from the others? Which ones?
   - Are these mounts underdeveloped, well developed, or overdeveloped?
   - What does this tell you?
2. Now move around your palm, assessing each of the nine mounts. Start with the passive hand and move on to the active hand. Note for both hands the development of all mounts and any special features, such as markings or a line ending on a mount.
3. Review this chapter and assess your character through the mounts. Once you have done so with confidence, you can move on to assessing a friend or family member. Use the different methods outlined in this chapter, such as looking across the palm and using your fingertips to feel the mounts, in order to assess their firmness.
4. What are three lessons you have learned from assessing the mounts on your palms? How can you apply these lessons to bettering your life?
5. What are three concrete steps that you can take right now to ensure that you are a well-balanced, happy individual?
6. Think about the advice that you could offer to a subject based on a reading of his mounts. How can the mounts help pinpoint our best direction in life?

CHAPTER SIX

THE THUMB

Discover the special meanings of the thumb. What are the features of the thumb?
How does the thumb reveal aspects of a personality?

The importance of the human thumb is undeniable. It is the opposable thumb that sets us apart from all other species. While some primates do have a thumb, it cannot be used to grasp objects in the same way ours can—it is the thumb that gives us the ability to write, draw, use tools, and be creative. The thumb side of the hand is known as the **radial**, or active, side of the hand.

Some ancient palmists, such as those from Hindu and gypsy cultures, considered the thumb to be such an important aspect of palmistry that they believed a full assessment could be made of a person's character by examining this digit alone. Palmists from more modern times, such as Cheiro (see page 15), have also agreed on the relevance of the thumb and have devoted much attention to it in their writings, while others have rated it barely worth a mention and have allocated only a passing paragraph to this significant feature.

The thumb represents the will and as such is an important aspect of palmistry because it demonstrates an integral part of our nature and indicates how we navigate our path through life. The length, width, and setting of the thumb all reveal minute details about the personality.

ASSESSING THE THUMB

Assessing a thumb may seem difficult at first, since there are so many factors to take into consideration. It is only when you have looked at a number of hands that you will be able to assess someone's thumb at a glance. The first few times, you may spend so long trying to figure out whether the thumb is wide or low-set, or even assessing the shape of the tip, that it may seem impossible to gain any understanding of this digit.

Use any opportunity you can to observe the way people hold their thumbs naturally and unself-consciously at rest. Public transportation is useful in this regard, as are other situations where one has to wait, such as a line at a grocery store. A person who holds the thumb tightly against the fist is likely to be a very guarded individual who cannot deal very well with confrontation. Conversely, a person with a broad spread of the thumbs and fingers is likely to be very open.

When you look at both thumbs, you will often find variations between the two. For example, some people will have a weak thumb on one hand and a strong thumb on the other. If the strong thumb is on the active hand and the weak thumb is on the passive, it means that the person will ultimately be strong enough to assert her will in any situation. If this is reversed, then the person will find it extremely difficult to put any ideas into action.

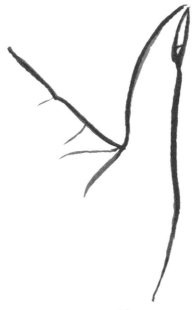

THE PHALANGES

There are three phalanges, or sections, on the thumb and each represents a different aspect of the person.

- The top, or first, phalange represents will.
- The middle phalange indicates logic.
- The third phalange (the mount of Venus) shows the way we feel about love.

Ideally, all three phalanges should be of equal length; this represents a balance in will, logic, and love, although by nature the mount of Venus tends to be a little larger than the other two phalanges. If one phalange is longer than the other phalanges, the person will put more energy in this area than the others.

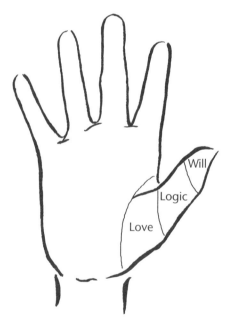

THE FIRST PHALANGE

The first phalange reveals the strength of our will and our determination to get ahead in life. The ideal first phalange will therefore be of a good size, strong, and well shaped. If this phalange is smaller than the others, it will signify a person of malleable character, one with little sense of her own identity. A person with a small first phalange, lacking her own ideas, is willing to coast through life.

Alternatively, if the tip of the thumb is large and misshapen, this could indicate that the person's will is so strong that she may behave like a bully. The most extreme example of this is the clubbed or "murderer's" thumb, seen on a person who tries so intensely to have her own way that violence can result—hence the term "murderer's thumb." This thumb type is very rare and, if seen, is not usually in evidence on both hands. Often it will be on the passive hand, indicating that the person has managed to overcome her behavioral difficulties. This type of thumb is not to be confused with a standard large-tipped thumb— it is unmistakable when you do see it. In fact, it resembles a thumb you might see in a cartoon after this digit has received a blow with a hammer. Proceed with caution if doing a reading for anyone with the clubbed thumb on the active hand, since this person's behavior can be quite unpredictable.

If the tip of the thumb is flat rather than rounded, the subject may be prone to insecurities, with little faith in her own abilities. A person with this feature may be weak-willed and change opinions in accordance with the views of others. People with this feature should be encouraged to work on their self-esteem and to believe that their ideas are just as valid and important as the ideas of those around them.

When the tip of the thumb looks as if it is bending backward, this is the sign of generosity of character. This person makes a genial friend. However, if the tip is too flexible, then the subject needs to be cautious of extravagance in the form of either spending too much or giving too much of the self to others. If the tip is rigid or inflexible, then a miserly attitude will prevail. People with this feature may give nothing of themselves or their money.

People who have a squared-off look to the tip of the thumb are likely to be realists who tend to take on too much, particularly at work, where they may find it difficult to delegate. A conic-tipped thumb reveals a creative type with a tendency to become overexcited. The spatulate tip reveals a talent with the hands, while the pointed tip is the thumb of the idealist. A fleshy, thick tip reveals a person with a large appetite, whose temper may come fast and furious with anyone who stands in her way, either at the buffet or in the boardroom.

THE SECOND PHALANGE

The second phalange indicates logic, an essential requirement for rational thought and action. Therefore, the ideal length of the middle phalange of the thumb is the same length as the top and bottom phalanges; ideally, too, this phalange should be very slightly slimmed in relation to the tip. A thick second phalange reveals the tendency to try to force opinions onto others, and a thin second phalange indicates a weak, timid character with a delicate nature. A waisted thumb, where the middle phalange curves slightly inward in the middle, is the sign of a natural diplomat—a person blessed with tact.

When the second phalange is short in relation to the other phalanges, this indicates a person with little logic who will plunge into situations headlong with absolutely no thought of the consequences. It indicates someone who is quick with her opinions and only ever sees one side of the story, and needs to learn the value of slowing down and thinking before acting.

A long second phalange, however, reveals a person who spends so much time pontificating on a subject that she will never get around to doing anything. Such a person will never seem to take a firm stance on anything, but will seem happiest when agreeing with both sides of every argument.

THE THIRD PHALANGE

The mount of Venus is considered the third phalange, so all that is applicable to this mount in the previous chapter also applies here (see pages 86–87). However, when doing a reading it is important to realize that the mount of Venus is actually a part of the thumb—this mount is located where the thumb joins the hand. If this phalange is of similar length to the other two joints, balance is indicated. If the third phalange is longer, the person is likely to be extravagant and impetuous. If it is shorter, then you will find a person who tends to think before she acts.

WORKBOOK EXERCISES

If there is an imbalance in the thumb, you can expect it to have a significant impact on a person's life. The thumb is a dominant digit and as such plays a significant role in the way we live our lives. Subsequently, if any of the phalanges of the thumb are either smaller or larger than the others, you can expect that the area it represents takes a less or more important role in that person's life. Following are exercises that can be undertaken to help balance any limitations in the thumb.

1. If the first phalange (the tip) is small or weak, this person may find it difficult to get motivated, or she may feel that her opinions have less value than those of others. To overcome this, a person with a lack of motivation needs to write out a concrete plan and make sure that every day she takes steps toward ensuring that this comes to fruition. If the person lacks confidence in her opinions, then the first thing she should do is to find a topic that she has a passion for, form a solid opinion on it, and then tell a close friend her feelings on the subject in a strong and positive manner. This will help her gain the confidence she needs to express her opinions.

2. If it's the logic (second) phalange that is weak, then this person needs to ensure that she always steps back and thinks about what she plans to do before she does it.

3. When it's the mount of Venus that needs building, then finding a passion and living it is the way to go. Each of us has some desire, some dream that we yearn for—and we may have to cast our minds back to a childhood dream before we find it. Finding that dream and allowing ourselves to live it, to immerse ourselves in it, and feel true passion can help us feel truly fulfilled. No excuses, start now—do it for yourself.

SETTINGS OF THE THUMB

There are three settings for the placement of the thumb: high, low, and middle. The middle-set thumb starts halfway down the palm, midway between the base of the index finger and the wrist. The person with the middle-set thumb is likely to be straightforward, easygoing, and well balanced.

- The high-set thumb is nearer to the index finger, and indicates the creative soul who may tend to bend the rules as far as possible without breaking them.
- The thumb set low down on the hand reveals independence and creativity. The closer the thumb is to the wrist, the stronger these characteristics may be.
- It is a good idea also to consider the angle at which the thumb juts out from the palm. Generally speaking, the average thumb will extend from the palm at an angle of around

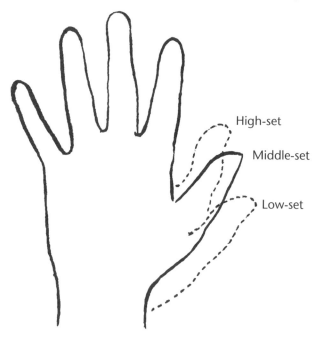

High-set

Middle-set

Low-set

forty-five to ninety degrees. If the angle is smaller than this, the person may be unduly cautious and guarded; a wider angle could indicate extravagance in nature and actions.

- When a low-set thumb is combined with a wide angle, you can expect an unconventional individual. This is not a person who is inspired by the mundane—she will need adventures such as climbing mountains and exploring uncharted terrain.
- Contrast this with a high-set thumb combined with a narrow angle. The person with this feature may be somewhat contradictory—creative yet cautious, inspired yet guarded. This is a challenging combination.
- The thumb that is held close to the palm indicates someone who is not inclined to take risks. People with this feature will often keep their feelings to themselves, and if they actually hide the thumb within the palm or under the other fingers, you can be sure they are feeling extremely uncomfortable. Such people are often out of their depth in almost any social situation and have difficulty relating to other people; often they are emotionally immature.
- People with thumbs held at a wide angle from the palm are adventurers. They usually seek more than their immediate environment can offer and cannot be tamed into a sedate nine-to-five existence. These people have no idea of their limits and will take on far too much, only to be disappointed when things do not work out the way they had hoped. They will not be downcast by failure for long, however, and will move happily on to the next challenge.

 WORKBOOK EXERCISES

1. At a glance, can you figure out the setting of your thumb? Does a closer inspection reveal a different tale?
2. What does the setting of your thumb reveal about you?
3. Take a look at the settings of the thumbs of people you know well. Are you surprised by the thumbs' settings or was it what you expected considering their characters?

THE LENGTH OF THE THUMB

To determine the length of the thumb, hold it against the side of the palm and assess its length in relation to where it reaches on the Jupiter (index) finger. A thumb of normal length will come halfway up the third phalange of this finger. Another way of measuring the thumb is to measure the length of the first two phalanges in relation to the little finger—ideally, these should be of equal length.

Take into account the setting of the thumb when assessing its length. A low-set thumb can appear short when measured against the Jupiter finger, so in this case it is best to use a ruler to compare it to the Mercury finger. A long thumb shows a natural leader, a person with a commanding presence who can take control in any situation. However, a long thumb accompanied by a long first phalange can mean that positive leadership qualities are hidden beneath a bullying, brutish manner.

People with a short thumb may lack motivation, particularly if the thumb is also thin. They may wait for excitement to come to them rather than seeking an interest in life. They will often think that the world owes them a favor and may be quick to complain about the way they are treated. People with this feature are best advised to learn to think for themselves and take the initiative if they wish to achieve success.

The width of the thumb is important. For example, if a thumb is long but thin, the person may be a dreamer rather than someone who is able to take control; someone with original ideas who does not know how to put them into practice.

A thick thumb is a positive feature, particularly when it is also long. This is a sign of a strong character, with a powerful sense of purpose.

A short, thin thumb, on the contrary, may show a meek and passive person, one who needs to learn to stand up for herself.

A short, thick thumb shows a person with stamina and tenacity who will work relentlessly in an effort to get to the top.

OTHER FEATURES OF THE THUMB

FLEXIBILITY

When examining the thumb, lightly take it in your hand and move it around, forward, backward, and in a clockwise and counterclockwise direction. A thumb that moves readily is deemed flexible. A person with a flexible thumb is likely to be open-minded, willing to listen to the opinions of others, and adaptable in almost any situation.

An inflexible or rigid thumb is one that is almost immovable and indicates a person with this nature, one with opinions that she will adhere to at all costs, regardless of any evidence to the contrary. On the positive side, people with rigid thumbs tend to be very reliable and make responsible employees who will remain loyal to their employers.

A thumb so flexible that it appears to be loose in its socket indicates a person with almost no beliefs of her own. Such a person will rarely offer an opinion and will be very easily swayed.

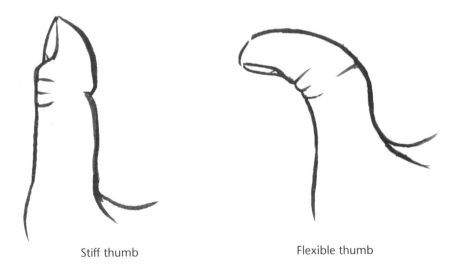

Stiff thumb   Flexible thumb

THE THUMBNAIL

Often, the shape of the thumb will dictate the shape of the thumbnail. When assessing the shape of the nail, ignore the white tip and just examine the pink nail bed itself.

  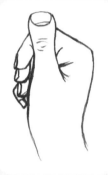

- Long, almond-shaped nails are usually found on conic and psychic fingers and thumbs. These shapes indicate a refined person with a love of beauty and creative talent.

- Square nails are the sign of a hard worker who is willing to achieve success through diligence and perseverance.

- Wide, short nails are the sign of a person who tends to be really critical of her own abilities. It is difficult to convince this type of person that she has done a good enough job.

- A short thumbnail is more likely to be found on a clubbed thumb and can indicate a person with a short temper and a limited attention span.

THE HALF-MOONS

The presence of the white **half-moons** at the base of the fingernails is a positive sign, as it indicates good health. However, even more auspicious is the presence of half-moons on the thumbs only and not on any other fingers. A person with this feature will be blessed with good luck.

Naturally, the presence of the half-moons is also dependent on grooming. Well-manicured fingers and thumbs with the cuticles pushed back are far more likely to reveal a half-moon than are unkempt fingers and thumbs. This should be taken into account when you are looking for half-moons on the nails.

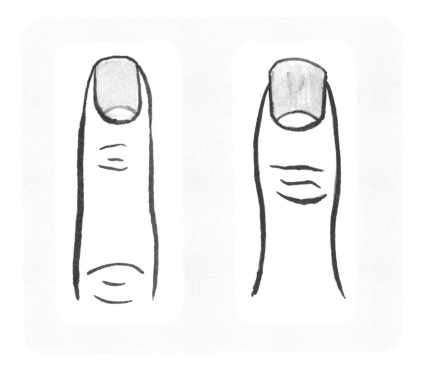

REVIEW

The thumb is a very important part of the hand. In ancient times rulers used thumbprints, imprinted on wax, as a means of sealing documents. Even now we use the "thumbs up" sign as a way of indicating that everything is OK.

The thumb allows us to assess many aspects of a person:
- **first phalange** (the tip): will
- **second phalange** (the middle): logic
- **third phalange** (the mount of Venus): love

Ideally, all three phalanges should be similar in length, although by nature the mount of Venus tends to be a little larger than the other two phalanges. If one is significantly larger, too much attention is paid by the person to that specific area—to the detriment of the others.

In the thumb we can read dedication to the career and to life. It is possible to assess what kind of manager or employee a person is likely to be by looking at their thumb.

The way we hold our thumbs reveals a great deal about our nature. Thumbs held close to the palm will point to the introvert who shares little; when the thumb is held widely apart from the rest of the hand, you will be dealing with an extrovert who shares everything with abandon.

WORKBOOK EXERCISES

In order to gain a sound understanding of the thumb, it is important to study it in depth. Select three friends or relatives on whom to perform this exercise. For each of the subjects, answer the following for both hands:

1. What is the shape of the thumb?
2. What is the length of the thumb?
3. Are any of the phalanges dominant? Which phalange?
4. Is the thumb set high, low, or in the middle?
5. What is the shape, size, and color of the thumbnail? Are half-moons present?
6. How flexible is the thumb?

Once you have done this, copy the worksheet below into your journal and complete it for all of your subjects.

Palmistry Worksheet

Name: . . . . .Age: . . . .

Hand shape: . . . . .Handedness (right or left): . . . .

Active hand: . . . .

1. Thumb shape . . . .

2. Thumb length . . . .

3. Dominant phalange . . . .

4. Thumb setting . . . .

5. Thumbnail shape, half-moons . . . .

6. Flexibility . . . .

Do the same for the passive hand.

Once you have studied fingernail color (see page 154), make notes about your subjects' thumbnail colors as well.

In your journal, record what you now know about your subjects' characters through the study of their thumbs.

CHAPTER SEVEN

THE FINGERS

Learn about the fingers, their features, and what they reveal in a reading.

When you really want to get to know someone, take a close look at his fingers. As we have already seen, you can judge a great deal from the hand shape, the mounts, the lines on the hand, and the thumb. In this chapter, you will learn that the true basis of the character is all there in the eight digits.

Each of the fingers, like the mounts, has a name that corresponds with a Greek or Roman deity. This name indicates that the finger has traits common to those associated with the deity whose name it bears. The Saturn, or middle, finger is the "serious" finger, balancing the dynamism of Mercury and Jupiter and the creativity of Apollo.

When you start to examine the fingers of your subjects, have them hold their palms facedown on a surface in front of them. Then get them to raise their fingers in the air. This is a good way to assess how the fingers are held. Some people keep their fingers held tightly together, while others splay them all apart. Sometimes, a finger will cling to the one beside it; another may stand aloof from all the others. This chapter will reveal the meaning of each of these features and show how you can gain a deeper understanding of a person just by looking at their fingers.

Look at each finger individually and assess how it relates to the others. Also, note how the relevant fingers on the active and passive hands differ. Whenever you are trying to understand some aspect of a finger, use your common sense. For example, some books say that the fingers should be the same length as the palm, but as palms vary widely in their size this is not an accurate measure. After you have seen a few hands, you will readily pick the long fingers from those of normal length.

Do not forget to ask questions along the way. It is important to note if knotty joints are a result of arthritis or if a finger is bent because of an unset break, as this makes an enormous difference in a reading. Some people also may inherit features such as very flexible joints and this will have an impact on the reading, so ask about these characteristics.

CHARACTERISTICS OF THE FINGERS

When examining the fingers, you will need to take into account the three phalanges, the length and shape of the fingers, the fingernails, and how the fingers are set on the palm. Fingers can be set on the palm in a straight line or on a curve.

Often, the first and fourth fingers are set a little lower than the others. If they are set significantly lower, this can indicate a person who lacks self-esteem and doubts his own abilities. When assessing the length of the fingers, it is important to mentally set them in a straight line, as this is the way in which you can assess their length in relation to the other fingers.

1) Spirituality and intuition

2) Turning ideas into reality

3) Desire for material objects

FINGER LENGTH

Generally speaking, those with long fingers enjoy attention to detail when completing a task, while people with short fingers like to dive in and get the job finished as quickly as possible. So if you want a job done quickly, find a person with short fingers, but if you want a thorough job, find someone with long fingers.

THE PHALANGES

Like the thumb, each finger has three phalanges. The tip, or first phalange, represents spirituality and intuition. The second phalange shows how well we put things into practice—or turn our ideas into reality. The third phalange indicates our appetites for the material things in life.

If the three phalanges on each finger are of equal length, the person is likely to be well balanced. If the phalanges are disproportionate in length, you can relate this disproportion to the characteristics of the finger on which the phalanges appear. This chapter will list and explain these characteristics. A short phalange will indicate that the person is lacking in whatever the finger represents, while a long phalange indicates that too much importance is placed in this area. Thin phalanges indicate weakness, while thick phalanges (particularly third phalanges) are indicative of overindulgence.

WORKBOOK EXERCISES

1. Consider the length and shape of the phalanges of your fingers. What do they say about you?
2. Do your phalanges vary on each finger or are they similar? What does this reveal?

FINGER SHAPE

You should assess the shape of the fingertips by looking at the palm side of the hand, otherwise the shape of the nails may interfere with your assessment. Look at each finger on each hand and note if differently shaped fingers appear on the hand. Note any similarities or differences between each hand.

The finger shapes share the traits of the hand shapes mentioned in Chapter Two:
- Square fingers are the sign of a worker.
- Conic fingers belong to creative people.
- Spatulate fingers show talent with the hands.
- Psychic fingers reveal the dreamer.

When the tips of the fingers vary in their shape, you can apply the characteristics for each of the shapes to the relevant fingers and consider the hand mixed.

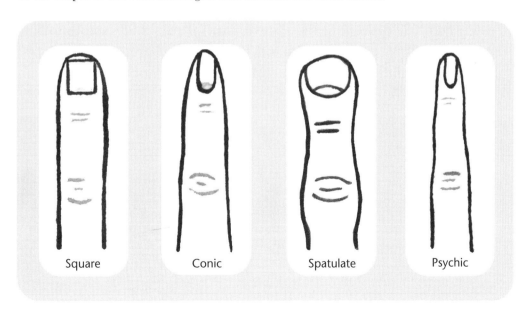

| Square | Conic | Spatulate | Psychic |

SMOOTH FINGERS

When the fingers are smooth, the nature of the subject will be versatile and easygoing. Long, smooth fingers are found on those who love detail and will happily spend hours working on a task in order to get it right. Short, smooth fingers are the sign of an impetuous nature. A subject with fingers like these will leap into a task with glee, but often abandon it before completion to move on to the next interesting thing.

KNOTTED FINGERS

When the joints of the fingers are knotted naturally and not through diseases such as arthritis, this is the sign of an analytical mind. Before this person acts, absolutely every angle must be examined from all possible perspectives. When the fingers are long and thin and

the joints are knotted, this is the philosophical hand—the hand of the philosopher. Often, people with these features are loners, spending more time studying than in social situations. More often than not, the person with knotty joints will be a worrier and their palms are likely to be crisscrossed with many fine lines.

THE JUPITER FINGER

The index finger is known as the Jupiter finger. This is the finger that governs success, the ego, and spirituality. The ideal Jupiter finger is of equal length to the Apollo (ring) finger. This indicates a well-balanced individual with a strong sense of self-esteem. A Jupiter finger is considered to be of normal length if it reaches into the top phalange of the Saturn (middle) finger.

When the Jupiter finger is the longest finger on the hand, this is the sign of a perfectionist and of someone with great confidence. When the latter characteristic is excessive, the need for control can often alienate others. The overabundance of confidence will often spill over into arrogance. A person with a long Jupiter finger will not take well to being given direction. He likes to give the orders, not take them. However, people with long Jupiter fingers will go far in life, as they know exactly in which direction they are headed and will let nothing and no one stand in the way of their success. They will always stand up for themselves and for any cause they feel strongly about.

A short Jupiter finger is one that does not reach, or barely reaches, the top phalange of the middle finger. When this finger is short, it signifies a lack of confidence. A person with this feature may be talented, but will rarely consent to being in the limelight. Acutely aware of the impression made upon others, he will never attempt to do anything out of the ordinary for fear of appearing foolish.

If this finger stands apart from the Saturn finger, the person will be independent; if it clings to the Saturn finger, the person may be jealous and possessive in his relationships.

When the Jupiter finger is pointed at the tip, this indicates a person with a deep interest in spirituality and religion. When the finger is long and pointed, the person may have an aptitude for religious leadership.

THE SATURN FINGER

The middle finger is called the Saturn finger in palmistry. It is the balancing finger, the sensible side of the family. This finger relates to responsibility, the family, and logic. On most hands, it is the longest finger.

The Saturn finger should stand straight, tall, and proud as evidence of a balance in life. Should this finger bend toward or cling to one of the fingers on either side, it indicates an imbalance in the person's life. If it curves toward the Jupiter finger, it reveals an outgoing nature, a person who revels in being around others. When it curves toward the ring, or Apollo, finger, it is an indication of a loner, a person who prefers his own company to that of others.

The ideal length of this finger is about a half a phalange longer than the other fingers. If it is longer than this, the person will find it hard to move outside his small social circle and will not wish to move beyond that comfort zone. A short Saturn finger is the sign of a person who will never live up to other people's expectations. The world will be promised, without anything ever coming of it.

A person with the Jupiter and Saturn fingers of equal length may be more comfortable when indulging in scholarly pursuits than in conversation—and this tendency is heightened if the joints are knotty. However, very little will come of all of this knowledge, as this individual is likely to keep all that he learns to himself. When the Saturn and Apollo fingers are of equal length, the subject is likely to be a great risk-taker and will often behave in a foolhardy manner.

THE APOLLO FINGER

The Apollo (ring) finger is related to success and artistic tendencies. When this finger is long, the subject will have great artistic talent, and when it is longer than the Jupiter finger, it is evident that the subject is extremely content with his direction in life.

When the Apollo finger is short, lower than the middle of the top phalange of the Saturn finger, creativity will be limited and you will find that people with this feature tend toward a pessimistic outlook on life. They will not stretch themselves artistically, believing that their efforts will always go unrecognized, and they will manage to find criticism in the most unstinting praise.

When this finger is long and straight and inclines toward the Saturn finger, it means that artistic qualities are boosted with a keen head for business. This is the hand of an artist with a knack for marketing—and the ability to market the self. People with this type of Apollo finger will have an understanding of the commercial aspects of their calling: they will know what sells and be able to create their work accordingly. If the Apollo finger leans toward the Mercury finger, this will show a person who makes a living from his creativity.

A long first phalange indicates creativity, but if it is overly long, then ostentation and pretentiousness are likely to dominate. When the phalange is short, it indicates an interest in art, but talent that is not commensurate. Such a person is likely to indulge in artistic pursuits for enjoyment only.

When the second phalange is short, you will find that the person has little inclination toward anything of an artistic nature, unlike the person with the long second phalange, who will be blessed with a unique artistic talent.

A long base phalange is a sign of a person for whom material needs take precedence over spiritual or creative needs. Such a person will happily channel his talents into earning money, regardless of whether the work is interesting or fulfilling. The short base phalange is indicative of a person with little to no interest in the arts. If all phalanges are the same length, this indicates balance in all areas.

SPECIAL MARKINGS

The **ring of Solomon** encircles the base of the Apollo finger and, if present, is an indication that the person has great spiritual potential. The name derives from the ring of King Solomon, a powerful device that enabled him to communicate with animals. People with this marking are very sensitive to the needs of others and are often found in humanitarian occupations.

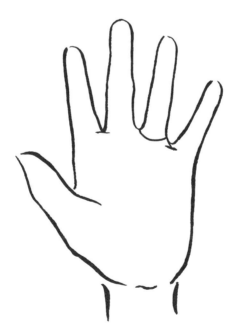

THE MERCURY FINGER

The Mercury finger, though the smallest, certainly packs a lot of energy into a small space. It is the one that is most likely to reveal a person's aptitude for success. If the finger has straight lines, free of kinks and curves, success is most likely.

Judging the length of the Mercury finger can be difficult, as this finger is more likely than the others to be low-set, making it appear shorter than it actually is. Use a ruler to be sure and only assess fingers on the same hand.

A Mercury finger is a good length if it comes up to the top phalange of the Apollo finger. A Mercury finger of normal length shows a person with good communication skills and positive self-confidence. A short Mercury finger is the sign of a poor communicator and a person who lacks confidence. If the Mercury finger reaches the nail of the Apollo finger, then it is considered long. The person with a long Mercury finger is a highly skilled communicator who instinctively knows the correct social and business behavior in any situation.

Should this finger be low-set, it indicates the person's lack of confidence in his own abilities. While people with this feature are usually intelligent, they will often be afraid to speak their mind for fear of upsetting other people. They tend to be followers in conversations rather than leaders.

The person who holds the Mercury finger apart from the other fingers has an independent mind. Interestingly, a teenager's Mercury finger will often start to stand apart from the others just when he is beginning to gain independence from the family.

A long first phalange on the Mercury finger in relation to the other two phalanges on this finger reveals an intuitive, investigative mind, coupled with creativity. When this phalange is thick, it can indicate a person content with the simple things in life.

When the second phalange is long, success in business is indicated. People with this feature will have a real understanding of what it takes to fulfill others' needs. A short second phalange is a sign of loyalty, of the ability to be a true friend. If this phalange is thick, be aware that the person will tend to do whatever it takes to get his way.

A long third phalange is the sign of a person who has the ability to talk to absolutely anyone. A short phalange is the sign of someone who is easily led astray. When this phalange is thick, this could point to someone whose morals are questionable and who lives life with a different rule book than the rest of society. A thick base phalange also indicates a person with no enthusiasm and little creativity.

SPECIAL MARKINGS

Medical stigmata are a series of vertical lines under the base of the Mercury finger, indicating that the subject has a healing ability. People with these markings may be doctors, counselors, naturopaths, or even spiritual advisors. Such people would also be great gardeners or veterinarians, having a good sense with plants, animals, and all living things. If they do not make a living in this area, they will certainly spend their spare time in the garden or with their animals.

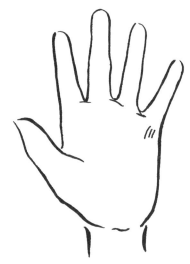

MORE ABOUT THE FINGERS

FLEXIBILITY

When the fingers are flexible, so is the nature of the person. He will be willing to please and will often go along with the crowd in order to keep the peace. Expect the opposite from someone with stiff fingers, however. Test the whole finger for flexibility, as flexibility between the middle and base phalanges is a most positive sign—a sign of a person with practicality and good sense.

THE FINGERNAILS

The ideal fingernails are those that are longer than they are wide and slightly curved. A person with long nails will be creative and drawn to the beautiful things in life. When the nails are naturally short, not bitten, this can indicate a self-critical person who is often impatient with the self and others. Narrow nails are the sign of a person closed to new ideas. People who bite their nails are usually nervous individuals with low self-esteem. Once their self-esteem is built up, the habit often disappears.

DROPLETS

If, when viewed side-on, the fingers appear to have **droplets** about to fall from the first phalange, this is a sign of extreme sensitivity. Droplets combined with a sloping head line indicate great creativity.

BODY LANGUAGE

Note how people hold their fingers at certain times. As we become more comfortable and confident in our ability to react well to a situation, our hands and body language tend to open up. When we are in a strange situation, we may cross our arms or hold our fingers tightly within our fists, hiding them. Watch celebrities at press conferences or presenting or receiving awards. You would expect them to exude confidence, but the way some hold their fingers will give you insight into the real nervousness they may be experiencing.

REVIEW

Serious or lighthearted? Creative or conservative? These are just some of the things we can read in the fingers alone. We need to assess the following when judging the fingers:

- **length**: Are they long, short, or medium?
- **phalanges**: Are they even or does one dominate?
- **flexibility**: Are the fingers rigid, flexible, or overflexible?
- **dominance**: Which finger is the longest? It is usually the Saturn finger, but if another finger is unusually long, this is the dominant finger.
- **how the fingers are held**: Are the fingers held closely together or splayed apart? Do some fingers cling to others?
- **their setting**: Are the fingers set in a straight line or in an arch? Is one finger set lower than another?

Also, assess the knuckles. Those with smooth knuckles are quick to come to a conclusion, while those with knotty knuckles are more analytical and tend to get bogged down in details.

Each finger has its own characteristics:
- **Jupiter**: spirituality and success
- **Saturn**: seriousness and responsibility
- **Apollo**: artistic ability and creativity
- **Mercury**: communication and business skills

WORKBOOK EXERCISES

This is an exercise in observation. Go to a few different locations and spend time looking carefully at the fingers of the people you see there.

- A library is a good place to start—and a place where you would also be more likely to find the knotty knuckles of the philosophical hand.
- When you go to the supermarket, observe the salesperson's fingers. Are they short or long? Do you find that salespeople with long fingers tend to take longer ringing up your purchases than those with short fingers?
- If you are at school, take a look at the hands of your fellow students and think about what their fingers reveal about them. Now look at the fingers of your friends. You will often find that their hands have many similarities to yours, more so when you have much in common.
- Compare your fingers with those of your parents, siblings, and grandparents, if possible. Do you share any traits with them? Have you gained new awareness about their natures based on their fingers? Or did you find what you expected, along the lines of what you already knew about their personalities?
- Looking at photographs of celebrities and others under the spotlight in magazines and newspapers can also be interesting. Check the business section of the newspaper for photographs of successful individuals. Where the hands of those featured are on display, you will be able to judge a few things from the hand shapes and fingers.
- Also, make a scrapbook by pasting images of different hands into various sections under headings such as Celebrity, Artist, Businessperson, Politician, Gardener, Musician, etc. Do you notice any common traits for each group? Until you build up a repertoire from many different readings, this is a useful way to familiarize yourself with many different aspects of a variety of hands.

By practicing in this manner, you will be building up your ability to read a person and consequently will become a much more effective palmist. Virtually anyone has the ability to do a hand reading, but to be a great palmist takes insight and ability and is something you need to work on in order to become truly skilled.

CHAPTER EIGHT

HOW TO READ PALMS

How do you perform a successful palm reading? Where do you start? What do you look for? How do you read a child's hand? The importance of gestures and body language.

The first palm reading that you should do is your own. Next, read the palms of close friends and family. When reading, make sure that you are relaxed and in comfortable surroundings where you are unlikely to be disturbed. Sit beside your subject, close enough to see the hands clearly and be able to touch them, but not so close as to make either of you uncomfortable. If one of you feels uneasy about sitting side by side, then sit facing your subject, but make sure that you are able to assess all the relevant details on the hands with ease.

STARTING THE READING

It is often best to start by telling your subject a little about palmistry, informing her about the kinds of things that can be read in a palm. During this time you should casually examine the subject's hands. Take her hands in yours, assess their shape, and test them for flexibility and color.

Make notes as you go, telling your subject what you are writing down. Most people will find information about themselves fascinating and will be intrigued at the wealth of personal detail that is to be found in their hands. Taking notes during a reading helps you to keep your focus, and a sheet prepared in advance will help you keep track of certain features—unless, of course, your memory is so good that it is unnecessary for you to write anything down.

While working methods are a matter of personal preference, it may be best for you to start by assessing the hand shape and then figuring out what feature stands out on the

palms. Look for one or more of these:
- a dominant finger
- a thumb that is the overwhelming feature of the hand
- primary or secondary lines that are noteworthy
- pronounced mounts

Also ask:
- Is the hand full or empty?
- What features dominate?
- Are the lines clear or chained?

All these questions should be answered before attempting to assess your subject. When you are just beginning with palmistry, it is best to do readings based purely on the shape of the hand and the primary lines. Virtually all hands contain at least the three main lines (head, heart, and life), and these, combined with the hand shape, can provide you with fairly detailed knowledge.

It is a good idea to deal with the primary lines early on, as most people's questions about palmistry are based on the issues revealed in these lines. It is easy to point out the lines and explain their significance. You can then quickly assess the fingers, secondary lines, and the mounts to help with your understanding of the person's character. Later in the reading, you can return to a more detailed study of these aspects.

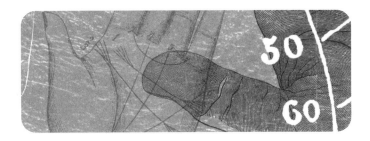

AIDS FOR A SUCCESSFUL READING

- You will need a good source of light when doing a reading. Turn the hand to the light if you need to in order to get a better view.
- A magnifying glass may come in handy when you are trying to assess fine lines, such as the children lines, which are often difficult to identify with the naked eye.
- You may also like to back up a visual assessment of some part of the palm with touch. It may be very helpful for you to assess the firmness of the skin and the flexibility of the hand as you proceed with a reading.
- Be prepared to ask questions as you go along. Some hands are so full that doing a reading can be difficult unless you ask the subject what she would like to know about and if there are any specific questions you should be answering in your reading.

THE ACTIVE AND PASSIVE HANDS

Start by examining the passive hand. Identify its shape and any outstanding features. You should then compare the passive hand to the active hand. Next, starting with the life line, make your way through the primary lines.

When reading the active hand, it is important to note how this hand differs from the passive hand and what this tells you about the subject:

- How do the two hands differ?
- What has the subject made of her life?
- Has the subject followed the life fate offered or taken an independent direction?

Note that children's active and passive hands are often quite similar. This is why it is interesting to keep copies of their palms over the years and note how they change over time.

READING BETWEEN THE LINES

As you become more adept at palm reading, you will find your intuitive side will take over and you will start "reading between the lines." To encourage this, place your thumb in the center of your subject's palm, using your fingers to hug the hand gently. Close your eyes and allow thoughts to flow into your head. With practice, more and more intuitive thoughts will come to you when reading a palm and you will rely less on individual aspects of the hand when giving a reading.

Be guided by your own personality when reading palms. If you like to talk, feel free to tell your subject as you go along about all the things you can see in the palm. But you need not feel pressured to say anything, particularly when you are starting out.

ENDING THE READING

Take as much time as you need before starting the reading, and do not be afraid to stop when you have read as much as you are able. It is always a good idea to end the reading on a positive note, such as "I can see a lot of success in your palm—you are destined for an exciting life," or "Things always work out well for you, and your love of beauty will ensure you will always find something positive."

READING CHILDREN'S HANDS

Children's hands have a lot of growing to do, but you can still see in a child's hand, from a very early age, the person she will become. The level of interest the child displays in a reading will depend on both age and personality. Many younger children will find it difficult to keep still for such a prolonged period of time, so you may find it beneficial to take copies of their palms and do the larger part of the reading from these.

Most of the time when reading for a child you will find you are directing most of the information to the parent, but do not neglect the child. Try to keep addressing her directly. Reading for a child has a number of similarities to reading for an adult, but it is even more important to take the time to explain to the child which line you are reading and what it reveals. If you refer to your own hand to show similar lines or compare the child's hands to the parent's to see if there are any inherited features, this will also entrance your young subject.

GESTURES

The way in which people use their hands is telling. While gestures can be a sign of cultural difference (note how many European cultures "speak" with their hands), understanding them is a good way to gain insight into your subject's personality.

Some people use their hands to give emphasis to conversation, with sweeping gestures, pointing, and much expressiveness. Others do not use their hands at all. It is interesting to note that most people will pay more attention to the person who uses the hands as an aid to communication. Such people will often be considered more interesting conversationalists than those whose hands hang limply at their sides.

People who point a great deal with their Jupiter (index) fingers often have an inflated sense of their own importance—and this is even more the case if this finger is unduly long. People who keep their thumbs hidden have a negative self-image, as discussed earlier, but the thumb may often reappear once self-esteem has been built up.

People who study body language often look at the hands for revelations of character. For example, someone who touches the nose frequently may be lying or trying to conceal something. Pulling on the ear can indicate the same thing. Watch your subject for gestures that may reveal more about his character. You may also wish to study body language to enhance your skills at palmistry.

CHECKLIST

When observing the ways in which people use their hands, take note of the following:
- Are their hands open or closed? Are their palms exposed (at rest or when active)?
- Do they keep their fists closed tightly, holding their fingers or thumbs within?
- Do they use their fingers to point or gesticulate? Is one hand dominant?
- Do they touch parts of the head and face when speaking, e.g., the nose or the ears?
- Are their arms folded or do they hold their hands tightly by their sides, or even sit on them, when speaking?
- What do these things tell you about the person?

REVIEW

The most important thing to remember when you are doing a reading is to be relaxed. Do not worry if everything you have learned suddenly flies out of your head. As long as you tell the subject that you are a beginner, she will be happy for you to refer back to your texts for advice and will be patient if you admit that you are unsure about the meaning of any marking or feature.

Make sure that you are sitting near your subject in a manner that enables you to see all the relevant features of the hands, and do not be afraid to move the subject's hands around. With palmistry, you really need to feel comfortable about what you are doing. As long as you feel content, your subject should, too.

Remember that you should never comment about aspects indicated on the hand that you do not feel comfortable about. You should always end a reading when you feel it is time. Always temper anything negative with a positive suggestion. A good palm reading should never make a subject feel anxious, upset, or worried.

Do not concentrate on one aspect of a person's hand to the detriment of another. You should always start with the features that leap out at you, but be aware of other qualities that may be quietly lurking within the palm, waiting to be revealed.

Refer to your own palm constantly over the years—you will be surprised at how much it can change. Make copies of your palms and those of friends and family and update them on a regular basis. This can be an invaluable resource.

WORKBOOK EXERCISES

This is the time when you will put together all the aspects from the previous chapters and do a full reading. Who will you choose for your subject? The person who has the honor of receiving your first full reading should be someone you know and trust, and who will be understanding if you need to look something up. Use the images on pages 190–192 for easy reference.

Prepare a worksheet with the following headings on it, in order to give some structure to your reading and to prompt you when needed. Simply remark on the various aspects of the features, pointing out anything of interest or relevance.

Palmistry Worksheet
Date:
Subject's name:
Age:
Handedness:
Hand shape:

Hand
Flexibility:
Skin color:
Skin texture:

Thumb
Setting:
First phalange:
Second phalange:
Size:

Fingers
Jupiter:
Saturn:
Apollo:
Mercury:

Mounts
Dominant mount:
Other notable mounts:

Primary lines
Life line:
Head line:
Heart line:
Fate line:

Secondary lines
You should have at least ten lines to note.

Additional comments

CHAPTER NINE

ACHIEVING A POSITIVE READING

Dealing with negative signs. The responsible palm reader. Learn how to answer questions about love, success, travel, and health.

NEGATIVE SIGNS

Sometimes you will be shown a palm that has negative signs in it, perhaps even indications of violence. Try to avoid mentioning any such negative traits and keep within safe limits by commenting on other, more positive areas such as the signs of a leader or an artist. Strenuously avoid any predictions of time of death. As mentioned earlier, this is not in the realm of the palmist. Also, remember that in a situation where someone approaches you to do a reading, you hold the power and have the responsibility that accompanies this.

That said, it is a good idea to point out areas of concern. If you see an island in the head line at around age forty-five, you could point out that mental stress could be a problem for the subject and that exercise, meditation, or other stress-control measures could help to prevent this.

If you do see a negative trait in a palm, choose your words carefully. Rather than pointing out that the palm shows the subject is aggressive, you could say, "You can be quick to react to situations, and need to take a deep breath and consider what you mean before speaking or acting." Also, suggest methods to counter aggression, such as taking up a sport to help vent excess energy or practicing relaxation methods.

When you see a problem in a palm, suggest a possible solution. If you see relationship troubles, point out the need for all involved in a relationship to work on it constantly. Make suggestions about the need to compromise and accept the partner's differences. Avoid at all times making your subjects feel that improvements in their lives are beyond their own control.

LOOKING FORWARD

Use palmistry positively to give those around you insight into themselves and new perspectives on enhancing their lives. Point out the importance of positive thinking and the great value of each individual as a unique being whose actions and creations can give others new insights. Remind your subjects that luck is a matter of perspective: those who are quick to feel fortunate will find valuable lessons in all that life throws their way. Show your subject that what lies in his palm is the story of his own ability to succeed, and that he can write the story himself by using the signs he has been given.

THE RESPONSIBLE PALMIST

The aim of this book is to create a responsible palmist, one who shares knowledge with others in order to enrich their lives—not to instill fear or mistrust. If any negative qualities are found, it is vital to avoid making bold pronouncements about them. Practice making tactful statements instead.

It is important for the palmist always to emphasize the positive. If you continually reinforce the fact that the subject is the only person who can bring about change, you will have learned to fulfill your responsibilities in the absorbing art of palmistry.

ANSWERING YOUR SUBJECT'S QUESTIONS

People often visit a palmist with several questions to which they want answers. The most frequently asked questions will be about your subject's prospects in relation to love, success, travel, and health. On the following pages are some techniques, learned as you worked through the earlier chapters, that you can apply.

READING FOR LOVE

Questions about success in the area of love will be the first thing most of your subjects will ask you. Many will ask if their one true love, their soul mate, is out there waiting for them. Fortunately, answers to questions about love are easy to find when reading a palm.

Looking at a person's hand will not only give you insight into the type of person he is, it will also reveal the kind of soul mate that person is seeking. It is always interesting to look at the hands of couples to see how compatible they are. Unlike the quizzes we find in popular magazines, this method involves little guesswork and the results cannot be manipulated by clever answers.

HAND SHAPES

Start by assessing the subject's hand shape. This will give you deeper insight into the kind of partner he will be most suited to.

THE SQUARE HAND This hand type belongs to the hardworking realist, someone who is practical and likes to get straight to the point in any situation. The ideal partner for the person with the square hand is someone who is also very down to earth. This person will quickly become impatient with anyone frivolous and will be greatly upset by a partner who is happy to spend money on new clothes or a DVD player rather than focusing on paying off the mortgage.

The square-handed individual needs a partner with a very similar belief system, someone who values home life and will be highly supportive of his career. The square-handed person will not usually want a fiery, passionate affair, preferring contentment and the security of a dependable partner. Check the heart line and the mount of Venus to confirm this. If these features are typical of the square hand (a straight heart line and an underdeveloped to moderately developed mount of Venus), you could expect the square-handed person to prefer the moderate course described here. However, if either feature is atypical or overdeveloped, then the heart could well lead the head and practicality could play second fiddle to passion.

THE CONIC HAND This is the hand type of the passionate individual, one who is often in love with the idea of being in love. Usually the heart line on this hand swoops broadly upward, indicating the extreme mood changes of the person with a romantic nature. Because conic-handed individuals are true aesthetes, they may often choose partners on fairly superficial grounds, such as appearance. However, their needs are much greater than this, and they also require intellectual compatibility. Consequently, they may often be sorely disappointed in their first few relationships when the reality does not quite live up to the image.

After the first few weeks of a new relationship, conic-handed individuals will often find that the partner's glamorous appearance conceals a dull mind or vastly differing political ideals. Subjects such as these should therefore be advised to take time to find out more about a prospective partner before getting romantically entangled. People with conic hands often jump from one relationship to another, with few backward glances at the old before they set their sights on the new.

THE PSYCHIC HAND Many palmists believe that people with psychic hands are fragile and will find this world too harsh. However, if such people have the right support network, they can achieve great things.

People with psychic hands would benefit from a strong partner, one who can act as a buffer against the more extreme aspects of society. It is important for a person with psychic hands to stay away from a relationship with another person with psychic hands. Two individuals of this type will tend to highlight the insecurities and more sensitive aspects of each other's personalities, and will come to rely on each other to the exclusion of all others.

A person with conic hands would ideally be suited to a person with psychic hands, as the former are creative individuals who would be a good match for the quirky psychic-handed person. The person with square hands may seem an odd choice for the psychic-handed person, but with compromise in a few areas, this can also be a very positive combination where the two balance each other.

SPATULATE HANDS People with spatulate hands are usually so easygoing that almost any of the other hand types will suit them, particularly other spatulate-handed individuals. The one requirement would be for another person whose love of activity matched their own. This is not to say that individuals with different interests cannot make a successful match, but people with spatulate hands may find that "those who play together stay together."

The relationships of a person with spatulate hands may be outside convention. For example, you may find such a person as half of a couple who have happily lived together for twenty years without marrying. This can also be a relationship of companionable silences, of sitting happily together and enjoying each other's company without the need for conversation. This is not to say that all people with spatulate hands are the strong, silent type—it is just that they do not feel the need to fill silences unnecessarily.

MIXED HANDS If an individual has mixed hands, you will need to assess the hand characteristics and check for details about these. For example, someone with a square hand and conic fingers could combine the personality features described for these two different types and may consequently have a number of differing needs from a relationship.

Heart line

READING THE LINES FOR LOVE

The first lines many subjects will want you to examine in your reading will be the marriage lines (see pages 68–69), but you will need to evaluate a few other things first. Once you have checked out the hand shape and know what type of person you are dealing with, and what kind of relationship will suit this person, you should then assess the heart line to see what it reveals. Read the palm to find answers to these questions:

• Are you dealing with a passionate individual, a realist, or a romantic?

• How chained is the heart line?

• Are there lines of influence arising from the line or do they drop down from the line?

Chained line

A chained heart line is quite normal. As you have read earlier (see page 47), this merely indicates the usual heartbreaks that we all suffer when treading love's winding path. An individual with no chains on the heart line is a rare individual. If the line is smooth, check if it is curved or straight and where it ends. Either this person has had no unfortunate endings to any relationship or he is not warm-hearted and previous relationships have had no impact. Another alternative is that this person has yet to have any relationship of substance.

Marriage lines

Now check the marriage lines. Ask yourself:

• How many lines are there?

• How long or deep are they?

• Where do they lie on the palm?

• How do they end?

Most marriage lines are quite short, around ¼ inch or less, while longer lines indicate longer relationships. A marriage line almost as long as the

The lucky M

heart line is extremely rare and bound to denote a relationship of immense significance.

Another formation to look out for is the lucky M (see page 76). If this is present, you can be sure that the person is destined for a successful and happy life partnership.

THE LOVE MOUNT

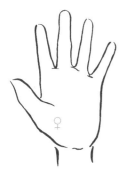

The mount that is most closely aligned with love is the mount of Venus and it is here that you should look to ascertain the level of a subject's passion. When this mount is flat, the subject will be quite lacking in passion, but when it is very prominent, lustful thoughts may often preoccupy the subject. A mount of Venus that is somewhere in between—well formed but not dominant, and firm to the touch—is the mount of the well-balanced individual with a healthy outlook on love, life, and sex.

OTHER INDICATORS

FLEXIBILITY Look also for flexibility in the hands, to assess how adaptable the person will be in a relationship. The subject with moderately flexible hands will readily adapt to another person in a relationship and will coexist happily with the partner. A person with firm or even rigid hands, fingers, and thumbs will be someone who insists on dominance in a relationship and will be unlikely to enjoy an equal partnership, finding a compliant partner more suitable.

A person with overly flexible hands is likely to be someone who is usually dominated in a relationship. However, it is possible that this person will finally have enough one day and end the relationship—without the partner ever knowing his true feelings.

TEXTURE The texture of the skin can also indicate how a person will behave in a relationship and it is another area where like should meet like. When the skin texture is fine, the person will be sensitive and romantic and will not be suited to the more coarse-textured individual. The person with coarse skin texture tends to say exactly what comes to mind without a great deal of thought as to how this may affect others. This person will also tend to have fairly basic requirements from a relationship. There is little need for sonnets, candles, and bubble baths to win this individual.

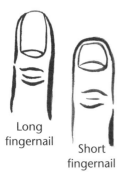

Long fingernail

Short fingernail

FINGERNAILS The person with long fingernails that are rounded at the tip is an individual with an open mind, one who is very giving in a relationship. However, if the fingernails are long but narrow at the ends, the person will tend more toward selfishness, not considering the needs of his partner. Short nails are often found on the hands of people who tend to be very self-critical and often this criticism will spill over to those close to them. Because of their lack of faith in their own attributes, they can drive lovers away with their negative attitude.

WORKBOOK EXERCISES

1. Do a reading for love on yourself, identifying the following factors:
   a) hand shape, b) hand features, c) flexibility, d) skin texture, e) fingernails, f) heart line, g) relationship lines, h) mount of Venus
2. Record your results in your journal. Do these results match who you perceive yourself to be?

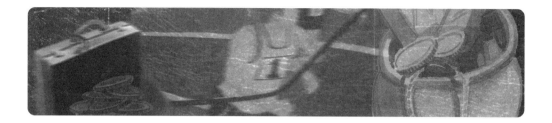

READING FOR SUCCESS

An important question for most subjects will be, "Will I be successful in my life?" Finding success in every person's palm is a major role of the palmist. Every hand should have some degree of success written into it—just what form it takes depends on each individual's definition of achievement. All of us have within us the power to excel—we just need the right guidance and the self-esteem to propel us on the journey. Finding the right signs for each of your subjects will give them the confidence to know that they can be successful. As a palm reader, you should be open-minded and avoid applying personal values when doing a reading. Try to be objective, focusing on what is important to your subject.

Look carefully at your subject's palm before making statements about the likelihood of success for that person. Gain as thorough an understanding as you can to discover what kind of achievement this particular person craves. Establish from the indications on the hand what the desired objective is; this may be a long and happy relationship, fame in the world of the arts, or reaching the top of the business ladder.

Each hand will offer diverse signs to assist you in helping your subject to identify the areas in which he may achieve greatness. Here are some clues you can look for as you seek answers for your subject.

HAND SHAPES

THE SQUARE HAND People with square hands are good at organizing, persisting regardless of the obstacles, and working systematically. Though there may be modifiers on the hands (unusual lines, mounts, or fingers) that point to different types of traits, in general the square-handed person is practical, organized, and reliable and will work his way to the top in the chosen area of work. Look for a line of the Sun that ends in a star under the Mercury finger. This is the surest indicator that success will come in the business field for this person.

THE CONIC HAND A creative, artistic individual, the conic-handed person will rarely be oblivious to the aesthetics of his surroundings and is likely to find success in the arts in some form. Areas in which those with conic hands excel are the traditional artistic fields as well as interior design, architecture, and advertising.

THE PSYCHIC HAND When the love of beauty indicated by this hand shape is backed up by other positive signs, the subject will enjoy working in fields such as cosmetics, interior decorating, or floristry. He may also be involved in the esoteric arts—for example, a person with this type of hand may be found working in an occult store.

THE SPATULATE HAND These hands like to create. To enjoy what he does, a person with spatulate hands needs a "hands-on" kind of job. If this person has the medical stigmata, he could be blessed with the talent of healing with the hands in areas such as Reiki or massage, or could be a medical practitioner.

READING THE MOUNTS FOR SUCCESS

Many palmists, in particular William G. Benham (see Further Reading, page 180), believe that the mount types provide the greatest insight into where a subject's talents and interests lie, and studying them will therefore help you uncover the ideal vocation for your subject. To get the best idea of which mount is the most prominent, hold the palm flat in front of your eyes and look across it to judge which of the mounts stands out above all others.

MOUNT OF LUNA If Luna is the dominant mount, the subject is a Lunarian and success may come through creativity and imagination. Lunarians are often great storytellers and if other positive signs confirm this (such as the head line that ends in a writer's fork on the mount of Luna), then you can be sure that this person's ability is bound to manifest itself in success in the literary field. Alternatively, success for the Lunarian may come through studying law or medicine, or teaching literature at a high school or university.

MOUNT OF VENUS If Venus is the dominant mount, it is pretty certain that the subject is sensual and open to all life has to offer. Venusians are pleasure lovers, willing to do whatever it takes to achieve success and attain all they desire. Venusians are also very empathetic and would do very well as Samaritans. They love helping others. Because of their charisma, they could also succeed as politicians—and would end up leading the ticket. The Venusian subject may also have a talent in music, particularly if the mount of Saturn is strong and the Saturn finger is long. This combination will mean a gift for composition.

MOUNT OF JUPITER If this is the dominant mount, expect the subject to be highly charismatic. Jupiterians are ambitious, make great leaders, and also have an intense sense of spirituality. You may find a Jupiterian high up in a religious order, as the love of religion runs very deep in a person with a prominent Jupiter mount. Jupiterians are also suited to a career in politics. However, their high morals mean that they often find the machinations of the political career a little too hard to bear, and they will often retire from politics before their time and become successful business consultants.

MOUNT OF SATURN A strong mount of Saturn indicates a person who is wise, balanced, and responsible. Saturnians can be found working for environmental causes or in the fields of computer technology or teaching. Engineering and mathematics will also appeal to them, as Saturnians have an innate ability with numbers. Money means very little to Saturnians, who do not generally equate success with financial reward. Having one of their own political treatises published, to their own satisfaction, would be enough for them. They do not need the acclaim of others, but require the enjoyment of a job well done in order to feel truly successful.

MOUNT OF APOLLO When this mount dominates the palm, the subject will have an uncanny knack for dealing with the public. People with this feature will be happy in anything they do, so long as they are relating to others. Apollonians are artistic, personable, and very intelligent. They could make successful radio broadcasters, particularly on programs where they can expound their own views. Stage acting is another career in which their resonant voices can be used to great effect, and business success is also highlighted for these individuals. In fact, Apollonians could succeed in virtually any area to which they turn their attention.

MOUNT OF MERCURY If Mercury is the dominant mount, then you can be certain that the subject's talents lie in business and communication. While some people may stumble and hesitate, lost for words, this will never happen to Mercurians. The reason for their success in business lies in their exceptional ability to relate to others and their considerable language skills. The Mercurian can succeed in any field in which oratory is required, such as law, counseling, or lecturing. This person could also have a career in the healing professions if a series of small vertical lines on the mount of Mercury (the medical stigmata) is also present.

MOUNTS OF MARS When both mounts of Mars dominate, you are looking at the hand of the fighter. Dominance of the Mars mounts does not necessarily mean aggression, but rather a person who will never be deterred and has the courage to face and overcome any obstacle. Martians are drawn to the military and the police force and can excel in the athletic field, too, both as participants and as coaches. And, drawing on the stereotype, you would also expect to find this feature on the hands of a professional boxer.

READING THE LINES FOR SUCCESS

To read success in the lines on the palms, look at these lines to discover in what situations the subject's success will be attained, and the timing for this success:

- the fate line
- the Sun line
- the head line
- the heart line

Fate line

THE FATE LINE To judge success from the fate line is usually quite easy, and most palmists use this line as an indicator of success. Identifying a successful fate line is reliant on two factors: its size and where it starts and finishes. A person with tenacity and drive will have a strong fate line starting away from the life line—this indicates success on one's own terms, not the family's. Where success lies depends on two things: the mount on which the line starts and beneath which finger it concludes. If the line starts on Luna and ends on Mercury, you have an imaginative communicator on your hands.

Head line

THE HEAD LINE This line will reveal how well the subject uses his intellect. A person who has potential but has a weak head line will probably never get the success he is destined for unless action is taken to stimulate the intellect.

Heart line

THE HEART LINE Passion is an important criterion for success. The person who expects life to provide everything he desires without doing anything to attain these benefits is unlikely ever to experience happiness or satisfaction. A person with a passionate heart line is likely to be bursting with enthusiasm about every project and will not lose heart if things do not turn out as expected. A person with an upswing on the heart line will be optimistic and enthusiastic and may actively seek success. A straight heart line is the sign of the pragmatist—one who knows what is required and sets about to do it without fuss. Through hard work and determination, this person will gain the reward he seeks.

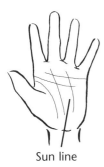

Sun line

THE SUN LINE We have already discussed the Sun line and how it relates to success (see pages 63–65), but if this line does not appear on the palm you will need to keep studying the hand. You will find the signs of success in virtually every palm you read. Remember that success means different things to different people, and to find it for others you may need to broaden your own definition.

WORKBOOK EXERCISES

1. Do a reading for success on yourself, identifying the following factors:
   a) hand shape, b) dominant mounts, c) head line, d) heart line, e) fate line, f) Sun line
2. Record your results in your journal. Do these results match who you perceive yourself to be?

READING FOR TRAVEL

To gain some understanding of the psyche of your subjects, ask them to describe their dream vacation destination—where they would go, how long they would stay, and what they would do. Travel plans reveal so much. During annual vacations, some may venture to foreign lands, while others stay at home and relax in comfortable surroundings.

Some people are naturally restless. Different places and cultures are calling to them and they never feel settled unless they are planning their next trip. However, despite our intentions, most of us just do not have the funds to jet off to Barbados every time we crave respite from the winter chill. Much of our need for adventure may be fulfilled in other ways. The more adventurous take up action sports that boost the adrenaline, some view documentaries on television, and others head to the library to read about other cultures.

If you look back into our ancient past, you will find that most of us are descended from nomadic tribes of some sort. It is only in relatively recent history that humans have been able to settle in one place on a long-term basis. Some people, however, still hearken back to these nomadic times, and you will see this clearly in their palms. The hand can reveal the inner restlessness of the person who relocates every year or so—the person who is off again seeking new adventures when the boxes are finally unpacked.

You will not see clear, simple lines on the palms of the restless person. He will have heavily lined palms with tiny markings deeply or lightly etched over almost every surface. The outer edge of the palm will be marked with little lines from the base of the wrist, near the mount of Luna, right up to the base of the Mercury finger. And it is these configurations that you would also expect to find on the hand of the avid traveler.

THE ADVENTURER

As you read more and more palms, you may meet an adventurer, someone who is constantly seeking new challenges and new places to explore. This person may have met up with other like-minded individuals and traveled the world with them, trekking, kayaking, and climbing in exotic locales at every opportunity. Adventurers' hands are distinctive, reflecting the desire for something different, and yet they still display standard characteristics. The hand shape is likely to be spatulate or mixed, with widely splayed fingers displaying the subject's individuality. A strong thumb is to be expected, with the top phalange (indicating will) prominent and well formed. If you can get adventurers to keep still for long enough to examine their palms, they will prove a fascinating read.

THE TRAVELER

The traveler hopes to add to life's rich tapestry through a series of experiences abroad—but not through extreme activities. The traveler will have a series of well-defined lines on the **percussion** side of the hand (the outer side of the hand under the Mercury finger), on the mount of Luna, and often above this. These lines may be long or short. Longer lines mean journeys of greater significance than shorter lines, but you should take the personality of the subject into account when assessing this. To a conservative individual, a long line may indicate a weeklong trip in another country, while on another hand this would reveal a yearlong journey around the world. A long line may mean a trip overseas for a month or two, or it could mean traveling one's own country for an indefinite period in a motor home. It is not the distance traveled but what the journey means to the individual that is important.

THE HOMEBODY

Some people do not consider travel a priority at all. For whatever reason, be it lack of money or lack of interest, some have no signs of travel on their hands. If they do travel, you can be assured that having a vacation is not the primary reason for the trip—they may be flying to a relative's wedding or traveling on business, but they will certainly not be traveling purely for pleasure.

HAND SHAPES

THE SQUARE HAND People with square hands are meticulous and love planning, so their itinerary would be planned down to the most minute detail. The square-handed individual would read all the guidebooks before heading off to the intended destination and would be able to tell you the best method of travel from one point to another, the restaurants offering the best value, and the ideal place to stay. He would have already purchased a phrase book if visiting a foreign country and would have learned the basics of the language before even packing a bag. Travel is usually important to those with square hands. They work so hard throughout the year that they really need their annual getaway and look forward to it with anticipation.

THE CONIC HAND Conic-handed people tend to be fascinated with foreign locales and when they travel they will either seek somewhere unique or the most fashionable resort. They have a very easygoing approach to taking a vacation—no careful plans are made beforehand. They eat out where their mood takes them, stay somewhere gorgeous that they just happen upon, and are soon sitting at little out-of-the-way cafés drinking with the locals.

THE SPATULATE HAND People with this type of hand tend to favor action holidays. The time spent away is more likely to be spent riding, climbing, or hiking than lying on a beach and soaking up the sun. If they are persuaded by their partners to go to tropical resorts, you can expect to find them windsurfing rather than sipping cocktails in the pool. While they enjoy their holidays, unless they are dedicated adventurers or travelers, they do not spend huge amounts of time daydreaming about the next trip away.

THE MIXED HAND As mentioned earlier, the mixed hand often belongs to the adventurer. However, depending on which characteristics are dominant, the subject with the mixed hand may display the travel tendencies of the more practical, plan-bound person as well.

READING THE MOUNTS FOR TRAVEL

MOUNT OF LUNA This is the mount that is most closely associated with travel, which is no surprise, as this mount is where most of the travel lines are to be found on the hand. People with well-developed mounts of Luna are travelers to the core. They will head off with nothing but a backpack and a smile, joyously anticipating their newest adventure. In contrast, people who have a flat or underdeveloped mount of Luna will be difficult to budge. You will find them reluctant to travel further than the local store. An overdeveloped mount of Luna reveals restlessness. People with this marking will rarely be satisfied with what they have and will always be looking for the next adventure. They will be plotting the next sojourn even as they stand on top of Mount Everest.

MOUNT OF VENUS Venus also plays a role in whether a subject is eager to travel. Because the mount of Venus is indicative of a person's level of passion, you can use this mount to help you assess a love of travel, too. A well-developed mount of Venus indicates a person for whom travel would enrich an already full life. If the mount is underdeveloped, the person may like the idea of travel, but would probably never get around to it. If it is overdeveloped, expect nothing but over-the-top behavior—the vacations of such an individual would be extravagant and full of overindulgences.

 WORKBOOK EXERCISES

1. Do a reading for travel on yourself, identifying the following factors:
   a) hand shape, b) thumb size, angle, and setting, c) travel lines, d) mount of Luna,
   e) mount of Venus
2. Record your results in your journal. Do these results match who you perceive yourself to be?

READING FOR HEALTH

It is surprising what you can see when you examine a hand for signs of health. We can read so much in the palm about it, ranging from genetic factors to environmental factors affecting our well-being. However, it is important to realize that a palmist is not a medical practitioner. We often play the role of counselor or adviser, but never doctor. Therefore, when you do see something in the palm, it is vital to reiterate to your subject that the markings on palms are never concrete, that everyone has within themselves the ability to effect positive change, and that medical advice should be sought for a proper diagnosis.

The important point the palmist can make is that regardless of what genetics has set out for us, we are ultimately the ones who decide on our destinies. When it comes to our own fate, we can either work toward attaining a state of optimal good health or, through negligence or bad habits, fall into a state of ill health. Remind your subjects that the advice you give them about checking on medical issues may be met with skepticism by some medical practitioners; few will be versed in the art of palmistry. Advise your subjects that if they have any concerns they could ask their medical practitioners to advise them on preventive measures for avoiding future illness, and perhaps seek out other practitioners such as iridologists to help pinpoint any specific problems.

When you read a palm for health, you need to acknowledge that no signs are permanent. So if you do see negative markings that indicate, for example, that a person is likely to be subject to vascular problems, you should stress that although the signs of illness may be there, it is up to the individual to take responsibility for his own health. Remind your subjects that this is the most effective way to make positive changes.

HAND COLOR

When you are assessing health in the hands, one of the first aspects to consider is the color of the palms. Regardless of race or skin color, many palms will fall into these color categories:

- **Pink:** A rosy shade of pink is the ideal color for the palm. It shows that the person is fit and has good circulation.
- **Red:** When the palms are red, the signs are not all good. Red palms can signify aggression, heart problems, and issues concerning the blood.
- **White:** When the palms are white with a bluish tinge, there is likely to be a problem with the circulation. To confirm this, ask if the subject ever experiences any numbness or tingling in the fingers or toes.
- **Yellow:** This can indicate problems with the liver and jaundice. However, it can also be a result of drinking too much carrot juice!

FIRMNESS OF THE HANDS

People with hands that are firm to the touch are often robust in health. They may rarely succumb to illness and will recover very quickly when they do fall ill. People whose hands are soft, however, are likely to catch every virus or may suffer from ongoing problems such as asthma, hay fever, or migraines. People with rigid hands do not fall ill very often, but when they do the illness will often be severe. Also, check the health mount by forming a fist and checking the bulge that occurs between the thumb and Jupiter finger for firmness. If it is full and firm, then the subject is probably in good health; if it is flabby, the person is likely to be unwell.

THE FINGERNAILS

Glancing at the fingernails from time to time will help to gauge our general state of health. Nails that are free of blemishes and pink, with a slight sheen, show a sound constitution. When we are worn out, this often shows in our fingernails—a slightly bluish tinge can reveal that a good night's sleep is needed.

- **White spots**: White spots or dots on the nails indicate periods of stress, not necessarily a calcium or zinc deficiency as popularly thought. Mineral deficiencies can show up in this way, however, so it is a good idea to examine the diet to ensure it is balanced.
- **Beau's lines**: These are deep horizontal ridges that appear across the nail, occurring as a result of trauma of some kind. They usually grow out as the nail grows, but if they appear constantly this is an indication that the person's health needs close examination. They could point to nutritional deficiencies, acute infection, or physical or emotional stress.
- **Longitudinal ridges**: These can indicate problems such as hyperthyroidism, skin disorders, and rheumatism—problems that are long-term rather than fleeting.
- **Mees's lines**: These are horizontal lines that run across the nails. If present, they indicate that the subject has experienced a high fever in the past six months or that they may be susceptible to heart disease.
- **Thin nails**: If the nails are thin and brittle and break easily, there may be a problem with the constitution. People with thin nails will need to play close attention to their diet to ensure they are getting an adequate intake of all the essential nutrients. Brittle nails can also point to thyroid problems.

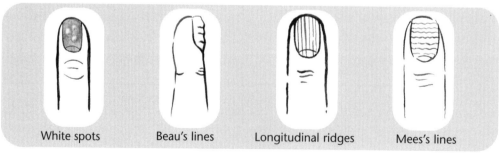

White spots   Beau's lines   Longitudinal ridges   Mees's lines

NAIL SHAPE

- **Short nails**: People with short, wide nails will often be critical of both themselves and others. They may have health problems associated with their negative natures.
- **Square nails**: People with square or rectangular nails often appear to be even-tempered, but their feelings are usually quite intense. Their health problems are often related to their emotions, as they may withhold their feelings to such an extent that when they do let go the effect will be explosive.
- **Almond-shaped nails**: People with an innate love of beauty characteristically have these nails. Such people are usually healthy and quick to overcome any illness.
- **Shell-shaped nails**: A nail that is narrow at one end and wider at the other is deemed to be shell-shaped. People with these nails are often quite fragile healthwise and may frequently suffer from one malady or another.
- **Concave nails**: If the nails appear hollowed out, resembling a bowl, be alert, as this can indicate a problem with the blood supply or with the glands (glandular fever, for example).
- **Watch-glass nails**: If the nails are convex, there are likely to be problems with the lungs.

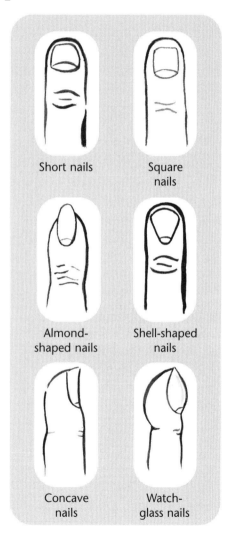

Short nails

Square nails

Almond-shaped nails

Shell-shaped nails

Concave nails

Watch-glass nails

THE MOONS

On each finger the moon should be slightly visible at the base of the nail. If the hands are untended, cuticles may cover these moons, and this should be taken into account—could you see them if the cuticles were pushed back? If the moons occupy too much space on the nail—a third or more of the nail area— a thyroid problem may be present.

THE STRESSED HAND

A hand covered with tiny lines and markings is what is known as a stressed hand. For people with hands like this, there is no time to fit in any relaxation. Such people are destined for health problems because they expend so much nervous energy. Check the head line on this hand for breaks and islands, as the ill health indicated by this hand will tend to be emotional rather than physical. People with stressed hands need to find the time to exercise and meditate if they wish to have relaxed and healthy lives.

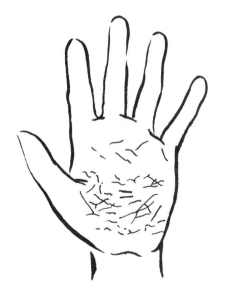
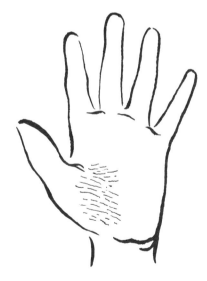

THE RECKLESS HAND

The hand of the risk-taker is often red and fleshy, with disproportionately large first phalanges on the thumbs and Jupiter fingers. A person with this type of hand will probably drive carelessly and at high speed, will have a love for the most extreme sports, and is likely to have a furious temper. The advice to this individual would be to slow down and proceed with a little more caution. If not, despite the strongest of life lines, this person could be extremely accident-prone.

THE LIFE LINE

A lot of information regarding our health is revealed in the life line. Islands, breaks, and tassels all have tales to tell. A break in the life line is indicative of two things: a dramatic change in circumstance or a serious health scare. Use the timing on the line to date the age at which this is likely to occur, and note that just as the body can heal itself, so can the lines on the palm. A break in the line is a warning that lifestyle changes are needed. These may include switching to a low-fat diet high in fresh fruit and vegetables, taking up forms of exercise that work the cardiovascular system, such as walking, or weight-bearing exercise to help build bone density, giving up smoking, limiting alcohol, and avoiding drugs.

HEEDING THE SIGNALS ON THE LIFE LINE

While we are not sure about the causes of many illnesses, there are some strong signs that lifestyle has some effect. Advise all subjects that it is best to do everything possible to avoid any risk factors (poor diet, smoking, excessive alcohol consumption, etc.). A tassel on the end of the life line may indicate that a life could end in confusion, ill health, or dementia. Remedial action would involve working the brain to ward off dementia and senility. Research indicates that reading, keeping up with current affairs, and doing a crossword puzzle each day can keep our brains functioning well into old age.

When the life line is long, clear, and deep, the subject's constitution is likely to be strong and it is likely that the body will be able to cope with most illnesses, whereas a person with a life line that is thin and weak is likely to suffer from ill health and be susceptible to disease. However, with a change in lifestyle, the life line can alter and become deeper, stronger, and clearer.

THE HEAD LINE

Issues with mental stress are indicated if the line is broken or if an island appears on this line. However, if a square appears around any such markings, protective forces are at work to help overcome any major problems.

THE HEART LINE

This can reveal illnesses of an emotional nature, such as a mental breakdown or nervous conditions. When the line is heavily marked or frayed, it indicates periods of emotional upset (usually in love), but can also signal a predisposition to depression or melancholy. Problems with the vascular system can also be signaled on this line in the form of red or blue dots.

THE HEALTH LINE

This is another area where it is possible to judge the state of a person's health, particularly in terms of long-standing problems. When the line is strong and clear, no physical weaknesses are indicated, but if it is fine or broken, there may be stomach complaints or problems with the intestinal system. People with allergies such as lactose intolerance often have feathered health lines.

WORKBOOK EXERCISES

1. Do a reading for health on yourself, identifying the following factors:
   a) health line, b) color of the hands, c) firmness of the hands, d) fingernails, e) life line, f) head line, g) heart line
2. Record your results in your journal. Do these results match who you perceive yourself to be?

REVIEW

LOVE

One of the main questions you will be asked when doing a reading is the love prospects for the subject. It helps to have a greater understanding of your subject so you can do an in-depth reading. Starting, as always, with the hand shape, gauge the person's romantic profile. This, combined with an analysis of a few different lines, can pinpoint the ideal type of relationship and the potential for attaining it.

SUCCESS

Everyone can be a success at something—from business to friendship. Finding individual talents on the palm can be one of the most enjoyable aspects of palmistry. Often, a subject will have disregarded an interest in a specific area, but once told that he has a special talent will take up the hobby with renewed vigor. It is the palmist's task to reveal that talent and encourage the individual to become as successful as he wants to be.

TRAVEL

Some people have travel in their bones, while others take a more neutral stance; it is usually for the former type that we do this reading. Typically, the more adventurous the person, the more daring you would expect his vacation plans to be. Travel lines are located on the percussion side of the hand and enter the palm from the outer edge of the mount of Luna. Generally speaking, the longer and deeper the line, the more important the journey. However, hand shape comes into play once again, along with that very important digit, the thumb. It is vital to consider the whole hand before making any assumptions about a traveler's journeys.

HEALTH

It is quite remarkable what you can see in the palm regarding health. However, when doing a reading, use the signals in the hands as pointers only and never try to give medical advice.

WORKBOOK EXERCISES

When you are really confident about your palm reading ability, you will be able to refine your talents by performing more specific readings on targeted areas. It really is best to start by looking at your own hand before moving on to anyone else's. This will allow you to spend as much time as possible familiarizing yourself with the possible features on the palm without feeling nervous or concerned that you are taking up too much of another person's time.

When performing a reading on yourself, it's important to step back and allow the information to speak for itself. In this way you're learning not to place value judgments on a reading, which will help you to become a more successful palm reader. When you are doing a reading, you should avoid dismissing a particular marking by thinking, "Oh, I'm not like that." Often, the palms will reveal hidden depths and talents that we've not allowed ourselves to bring to the fore. You should read your own palm as though it were the palm of a stranger and allow yourself to be informed and delighted by its revelations.

Once you feel confident that you are ready to undertake a full reading, choose three close friends to read for. When doing these readings you'll need to consider the following:
1. What are the dominant features of the palms and what do they say about each person?
2. What are their main strengths as shown in their palm and how can they best use them?
3. What are their potential weaknesses and how can they turn them into strengths?

Record the results in your journal and make a copy of their palms to review later.

After you've considered the results of your reading, ask the following questions:
1. How pleased was I with the outcome of the reading?
2. How pleased was my subject with the outcome of the reading?
3. What areas did I feel particularly strong in?
4. Were there any weaknesses in my reading? For example, did I stumble over certain aspects? How can I rectify this before my next reading?
5. Write down three significant successes with each reading.

6. Write down three aspects of the reading that didn't go quite as planned.
7. Devise a five-point strategy (based on your answers to the previous questions) to become a stronger reader.
8. Look at the sample readings in the following chapter and make your own impressions. What else did you see in these palms?

As you get more practice doing readings, you will begin to develop your own personal style. However, it is important to remember when undertaking a reading to avoid the following:

• Telling a person when he is going to die
• Bold pronouncements of ill health or bad luck—if you do see these signs, offer advice on how to avoid them
• Informing a person about the end of a relationship—you should suggest solutions instead
• Reading the palm of a person who is uncomfortable
• Revealing anything negative unless you can offer helpful suggestions and can balance it by offering two positive signs
• Reading the palm of a person in distress—make sure that he calms down before asking him what it is that he needs to hear and only then read if you feel it is in his best interest

Aim to practice reading as often as possible. You should try to do at least two readings per week to refine your skills. As you sit down to practice, reflect on the following words:

"The answers are before my eyes, all is written in the palm."

CHAPTER TEN

SAMPLE READINGS

Here are a few readings to show you how dramatically different some hands can be. What else do you see? Make your own observations, using the diagrams and notes in the book.

QUENTIN, **39**, RIGHT-HANDED

POINTS OF INTEREST
- Great differences between the hands
- Lines varying in depth of color
- Long thumbs
- Fate line starting in late teens

NOTES

Here is a person with notable differences between the passive and active hands. Quentin's left hand has far more activity than his right, but the most intriguing difference between the two is the way he holds his fingers. Note how his fingers are much more widely splayed on his left hand than his right. This could indicate that he has learned to keep aspects of himself in reserve until he chooses to reveal them to others.

Quentin's hands reveal why we need to consider aspects of the hands other than the lines when we do a reading. Because his palms are square, there are relatively few lines, but it's in the fingers and the thumbs where the interesting facts are revealed. Quentin's thumbs are reasonably low-set and are held far apart from his palms, indicating an adventurous nature. His thumbs are quite long, particularly when you consider that his fingers are short and wide.

This combination, along with the fact that he has a Sun line directly under his Apollo finger, reveals that he is assured of great success through much hard work.

The third phalanges on Quentin's fingers are thick, which reveals that he can tend to overindulge. This is also suggested by his fleshy mount of Venus. So long as this is balanced by a healthy lifestyle involving exercise and a sound diet, this won't be a problem.

Quentin's palms contain only a few lines, straight and short, just as we would expect from the square shape. What is interesting, though, is how deeply they are marked in parts. Quentin's heart line is quite dark during his adolescence, and then it starts to fade. At this time the head line starts to darken, showing that he started thinking with his head rather than allowing the heart to rule.

Quentin's fate line starts quite late—in his teens—revealing that until this time he really had no idea of what he wanted to be when he was older. However, he appears to be content with the path he has chosen and with the results that he has achieved.

Quentin's creative curve is much more pronounced on his active hand than his passive—he is making even more of this life than he was destined to.

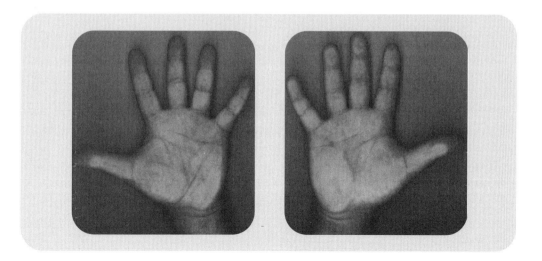

ROSEMARY, 63, LEFT-HANDED

POINTS OF INTEREST

- Head line sloping down quite dramatically
- Short Mercury finger on active hand
- Double life line

NOTES

Rosemary has conic hands, although her palms are more square than rectangular, which is what we would expect from a true conic hand. Therefore, we would expect Rosemary to be practical, with a good head for organization, which is balanced by her more creative, artistic side. Rosemary's life line curves out in a nice, wide arc around her mount of Venus, and to add to her luck, it is double (and tripled on her passive hand).

The most interesting feature on Rosemary's hands is the Mercury finger. On her right hand the Mercury finger is much longer than on her active hand. Also, on her right hand the first phalange is very long and wide. We can also see that her mount of Mercury is large—it almost appears to bulge out of the side of her palm on her passive hand.

However, in perfect juxtaposition, Rosemary's Mercury finger is very short on her active hand, and this is more noticeable because the setting of her fingers is quite straight. She holds her Mercury fingers well apart from the Apollo fingers. This indicates that she is a highly individual person, but at times has a lot of trouble expressing what she really means. She would be quite the contradiction—one day the office chatterbox, the next quiet and withdrawn. If she gains more confidence in her capabilities, we will see an alteration in both her Mercury fingers and her self-expression.

Rosemary has a very long marriage line, and if we look closer at the heart line on her passive hand, we will see a really short line from a relationship she had when she was very young. This relationship obviously had an impact on her, as it is still there, but it is not on her active hand, meaning that she has put it behind her. Her main marriage line is long and strong and still has a lasting impact. It is even longer on her passive hand, meaning that the relationship will continue to grow in importance and strength. It would be interesting for Rosemary to keep track of this line throughout her life, as it should continue to grow on her active hand until it reaches the length of the line on her passive hand.

Rosemary has a few travel lines on her hand, one of which travels across and meets up with her head line, which also joins to her fate line. This is an interesting formation and one that suggests that Rosemary's career could be tied to other cultures and countries.

Rosemary's hands are interesting, as there are widely differing features between the active and passive hands, revealing the importance of studying both when doing a reading. She has fewer lines on her active hand, indicating that she has managed to learn the art of avoiding stress whenever possible. Healthwise, there are a few problems shown on her hands—one in the past and one in the present. There is an island on Rosemary's head line around the time she was in her forties. She may have had a brief period of illness and, through a conscious lifestyle change, has put it all behind her. Her Mercury line is quite fragmented, suggesting digestive problems, possibly related to some food intolerance.

In short, Rosemary is creative, quirky, and very strong-willed.

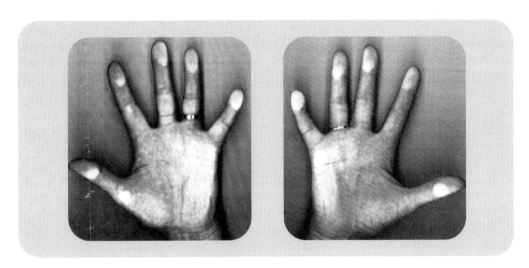

ALAN, 56, RIGHT-HANDED

POINTS OF INTEREST
- Very strong and dominant life line
  - Battle cross on left hand
    - Creative hands
  - Number of children lines

NOTES

Alan has spatulate hands—note the square palms and how the fingertips appear wider than the other phalanges. His fingers are thick and relatively short, indicating a methodical person who likes to do a job well. These are the hands of a person who likes to make things, creating with his hands, and we can be assured that every job he does is worthy of a master craftsman.

Note the thick, strong life line. It is so dominant that it almost seems to glow. On the active hand it starts out quite close to the thumb, but as Alan has matured and gained confidence it has moved well away in a wide arc. His head line is very long and straight, indicating a person with strong views and a finely tuned mind. Note how on the passive hand the head line almost cuts the palm in two.

Alan has a strong creative curve to the outside of his palm and it curves almost the full length, which is quite unusual. There is a distinct bulge at the bottom near the mount of Luna, also indicating a creative mind.

The lower phalanges on Alan's fingers are much thicker on his passive hands, which indicates that he knows how to keep his appetites in check. He may enjoy the finer things in life, but keeps a limit on how much he consumes.

Note how Alan's thumb is much thicker on his right hand than his left. He really is a person who knows how to get his own way. It is also interesting how much his left hand differs from his right. His left hand features a very long Jupiter finger, while the same finger on the right hand is of normal length. This could indicate that he was destined for an interest in spirituality, but has consciously moved away from any interest in that area.

Alan has a number of children lines on his palm, which is interesting for a man. Why this is particularly relevant is that while Alan has two children of his own, he has also taken care of his two nieces and a nephew from their early teens, along with a stepson and stepdaughter—and he has taken on this role willingly rather than passively.

Alan's fate line is interesting. It is reasonably well defined, but there are a number of paths leading from it, indicating changing interests throughout his career. His Mercury line is straight and clear, with a sister line pointing up to the Mercury finger. The presence of this line on this hand does not indicate health problems, certainly not in this robust hand. Rather, it is the line of the communicator.

In summary, Alan is thoughtful, creative, and an excellent communicator.

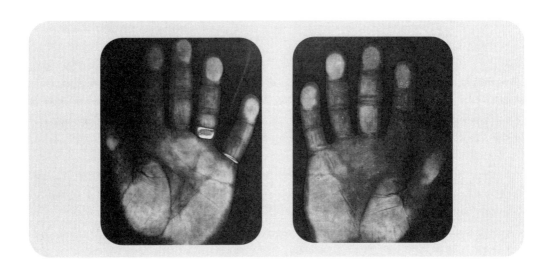

JANE, 43, RIGHT-HANDED

POINTS OF INTEREST
- Dominant Jupiter finger and mount
- Strong head line
- Interesting finger cling
- Lucky M and mystic cross

NOTES

The dominant feature on Jane's palm is the indication that she is a Jupiterian. Her index finger is very long and her Jupiter mount is very strong. This signals a very strong individual with a drive for success and a deep sense of spirituality. Note how the Jupiter finger on her active hand is almost as long as that of her Saturn finger, and see also how the Saturn finger is drawn to her Jupiter finger.

The cling of Jane's fingers is interesting—her Jupiter and Saturn fingers cling and sit wide apart from her Apollo and Mercury fingers, which also cling together. These fingers are trying to take some of the qualities of their mate, but none from the other fingers from which they are shying away. The serious Saturn finger seems almost afraid of the artistic side of the Apollo finger, so my suggestion to Jane would be to develop that creative side. She could try her hand at pottery or dabbling with some oil paints. Expressing her creativity in this way is something that she fears, but also something that she needs to do.

This is a hand of travel and adventure, with many journeys of great importance etched into the palm. The places that Jane travels to will be of emotional significance to her, which we can tell because of the importance they are afforded on her palm.

Jane's long, strong head line also suggests that her intelligence is a dominant feature of her makeup. Moreover, the fact that her head line is longer and stronger on her active hand shows that she actively works at sharpening her intellect, studying all the time, even if it is only through a daily brain workout with a crossword puzzle.

There are two strong marriage lines on Jane's hand, with the first relationship more deeply etched on her passive hand. As you can see by looking at the strong marriage line on her active hand, Jane has put the past behind her, and although traces of this relationship still linger, its importance has all but vanished.

Jane has two interesting markings on her palm: the mystic cross, indicating an interest in the esoteric arts, and the lucky M, which, judging by the other positive markings on her hand, indicates a great deal of luck with money and marriage. Again, this is something that she has worked to achieve, since she does not have the lucky M on her passive hand.

Jane's hand reveals a strong, intellectually sharp individual who has capitalized on her natural talents to become a success. She knows exactly what she wants and ensures that she takes every step necessary to achieve her desires. Jane needs to make sure that she spends a little time each day involved in some purely frivolous activity—something done just for the fun of it to truly balance her life.

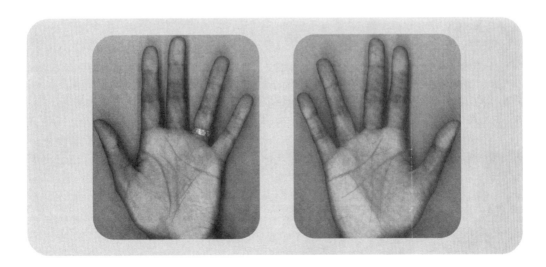

MARTY, 46, LEFT-HANDED

POINTS OF INTEREST

- Wide variations in markings on left and right hands
- Differences in finger spacings between left and right hands
- Saturn fingertip bent toward Apollo (more pronounced on right hand)
- Short third phalange on Mercury finger
- Long second phalange on thumbs
- Girdle of Venus

NOTES

There are marked differences between the left and the right hand, highlighting the importance of considering both active and passive hands when doing a reading. Marty's right hand has many fine, disjointed lines, with a heart line set well down on his palm, while the marks on his left hand, his active hand, are much clearer and stronger. This indicates a much smoother, more contented life than the one he was destined for.

While his hands indicate practicality, there are also many signs of a creative mind. Note the strong creative curve on the outside of the palm: it starts just under the Mercury finger and curves down almost to the wrist. This indicates a person with an unusual way of seeing things. Marty's perspective may be different than that of others', but will often lead to flashes of brilliance.

Marty's fate line starts on the mount of Luna, around his early teens, and heads up to reach toward Saturn. For such a unique mind he has taken a conventional route career-wise, but it would be surprising to learn that he goes about anything in the standard manner. That said, this is the fate line of someone who is happy to stay in one job from teenage years to retirement. He has learned a lot in this lifetime, as evidenced by the dramatic changes between his left and right hands. He has learned that in order to succeed a more conventional route is required. See his fate line's meandering and splintered path on his right hand—the line of a person with no real career path at all.

Once Marty reaches old age, he will take another route again. Have a look at how his life line branches—he may well travel the country in a motor home, which would be interesting, as he shows little sign of interest in travel at the moment. He is very logical—note how long the second phalanges are on his thumbs—but he tends to doubt his own ability at times. His Saturn finger is relatively short in comparison to his Jupiter and Apollo fingers, and on this hand this could mean someone for whom seriousness does not play a strong role. With a quick wit and a ready smile, Marty could certainly see the lighter side in almost any situation.

There is one very strong marriage line, which is forked right at the start, indicating that the relationship started, stopped, and has continued strongly. Below this, there is an earlier marriage line from his early to mid-teens, which has almost faded from memory and is possibly the cause of the chains at the start of his heart line.

Marty is fun-loving and could be mischievous. His hand is a very good example of a person who demonstrates the ability to make the most of one's life.

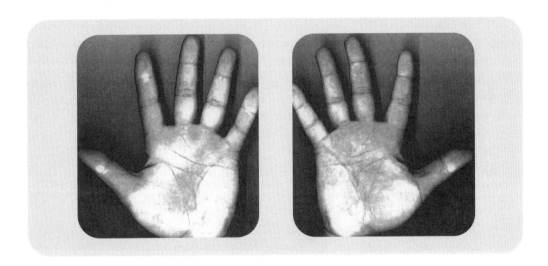

DYLAN, **30**, RIGHT-HANDED

POINTS OF INTEREST
- Double life line
- Broken fate line
- Long Mercury finger
- Prominent mount of Venus

NOTES

Not only is Dylan's life line long, strong, and widely curved, it is doubled. This indicates good health, but also luck. He would be the kind of person who seems to attract success.

The fate line is interesting on this hand. Note how it is joined to the life line at the start before moving away. Then, around the age of thirty, the line separates, breaking off into a new direction. This represents the fact that while Dylan's early career was influenced by the opinions of his family, he changed his mind around his late twenties and made the decision to pursue a completely different career.

Dylan's Mercury finger is long, and there is a wide spacing between it and his Apollo finger. This indicates a good communicator with views that are often unconventional but well reasoned. The first phalange on his thumb is long, which indicates that he knows what he wants and sets out to get it.

The dominant mount of Venus shows a person of passion and strong appetites, which are also evidenced by the thick lower phalanges of Dylan's fingers, particularly the Apollo finger. This indicates a person for whom aesthetically pleasing surroundings are important.

Dylan also has the family chain around his thumb, which is evidence of the strong ties he has with his family.

READING FOR A PERSON AT A CROSSROADS

Often, when it comes time to do a reading, you'll find the person in the middle of a serious change in direction, much like Dylan. He is thirty years old, and as you can see by the break in his fate line he is in the midst of upheaval about his chosen career. He is currently an engineer but is dissatisfied with this career path and would like to move to a more fulfilling job.

Therefore, we can help set our subject's mind at rest by pointing out other areas that may prove suitable. As you can see from this fate line, Dylan completely changes direction at this time in his life and the line takes another, smoother path.

Dylan is now studying mathematics teaching, an area to which he is suited for a number of reasons. He has long, thin fingers, revealing the ability to enjoy getting absorbed in subjects—and he would transfer this passion for learning into the ability to patiently teach. Dylan is exactly the kind of person that the teaching profession needs. He's intelligent (note the strong head line), he's passionate (as evidenced by his firm mount of Venus), and he has good public speaking skills (as shown by the mount of Mercury and Mercury finger).

Dylan needs to be encouraged to see this as a positive change, particularly as his fate line started off joined to his life line (revealing strong family influence in his career choice). He's an intelligent, committed man with a strong sense of social ties, so this change can only be viewed as beneficial for him.

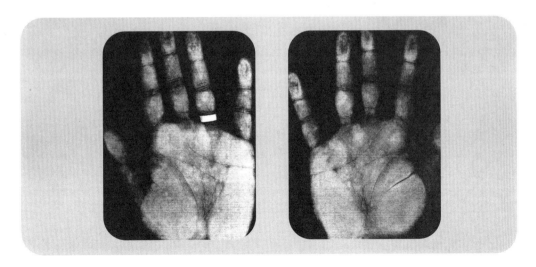

AVRIL, 45, LEFT-HANDED

SHELLEY, 45, RIGHT-HANDED

MIRROR-IMAGE IDENTICAL TWINS

POINTS OF INTEREST

- Wide variations in markings on left and right hands
- Differences in finger spacings between left and right hands
- Saturn fingertip bent toward Apollo (more pronounced on right hand)
- Short third phalange on Mercury finger
- Long second phalange on thumbs
- Girdle of Venus

NOTES

Avril and Shelley are mirror-image identical twins, which means that their identical features appear flipped, or in reverse. For example, the shape of Avril's right ear is identical to the shape of Shelley's left ear, and their fingerprints are the mirror image of each other. But as you'll see from this reading, Avril and Shelley are the perfect example to be used in a nature vs. nurture argument—over the past forty years each has adapted her life in such a manner as to become a striking individual.

While their palms display similarities in markings, the ways that they hold their fingers, and even the digits themselves, show that Shelley and Avril have moved in very different directions to become two quite different people.

Avril's fingers, while similar to Shelley's, are held apart from each other more than Shelley's, whose fingers tend to cling and bend toward each other. This indicates that Shelley doesn't have quite as much confidence in her own abilities as Avril does—Shelley relies more on each attribute to contribute to a whole, whereas Avril tends to feel more confident in striking out on her own.

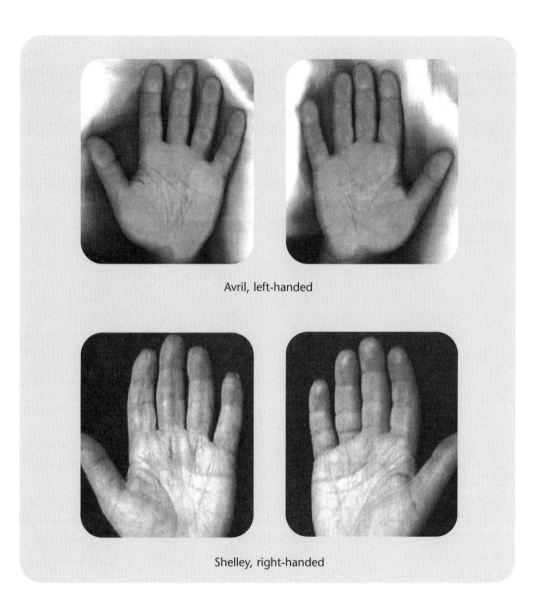

Avril, left-handed

Shelley, right-handed

Watching these two as children would have been fascinating, as their differences would have been evident even from a very early age—and yet there still would have been people who said, "Gee, how do you tell them apart?" It's my belief that being identical twins has left them almost as a positive and negative version of each other—where one would be outgoing in one area, the other would be introverted in the same situation. It is precisely these differences that has made them quite adamant in maintaining their individuality. It wouldn't be surprising to hear that their parents encouraged this individuality, or conversely, that parental insistence on dressing and acting like stereotypical twins inspired within them a desire to be seen as individuals.

Both Shelley and Avril are very creative—with an emphasis on the mount of Luna. They both have strong imaginations and can readily revert to a childlike sense of awe when they come across something they find exciting. These two have an incredibly deep bond and, despite any differences, will always know that nobody knows them better than the other.

While they share these similarities, Avril and Shelley will go about doing things in a very different manner. For example, if they were going to climb a mountain, Avril would tend to leap right in and just charge up, while Shelley would be more inclined to study the weather conditions, pack suitable supplies, and plan the best possible route. Shelley tends to worry about situations, while Avril has a more "whatever will be, will be" attitude.

Avril is left-handed, and when you examine her hands closely, you'll see a number of noteworthy differences between her left and right hand. What I find to be of greatest significance is the fact that on her right hand (her passive hand) the fingers are quite bent, leaning toward each other, with significant distortion on the fingertips. However, on the left hand the fingers are much straighter, although the Jupiter and Apollo fingers still tend to lean toward the Saturn finger slightly. Avril's fingertips splay out and as such would be classified as spatulate. When you combine this finger type with a few other items of note (such as the line of the Sun, which clearly runs up to the Apollo finger), you know that you're dealing with a talented individual who can try her hand at anything and achieve great success.

Note the makeup of the fate line—Avril has had a number of career paths and interests and this will continue throughout her life. She won't be the type of person to accept an early pension and retire young—she needs the stimulation and challenges from her career. Her Mercury line is short and straight, indicating that Avril is an exceptional communicator, able to get her point across without wasting any words.

Shelley is right-handed, and the most dominant feature of her hands is her thumbs, demonstrating that while she may appear as a woman with childlike innocence, nothing will stand in the way of what she wants. She's easily able to make people bend to her will, and nobody will ever resent doing her bidding. Shelley's hands are more complex than Avril's—there's a lot going on in Shelley's mind, and it is lucky she has the rugged health and strong intellect to be able to cope with such a manic lifestyle without it having ill effects on her life.

Shelley's thumbs have a spokeshave tip, unlike Avril's, which are more full, indicating that Shelley sometimes doubts her ability, which is surprising in someone who possesses such natural ability. Her Mercury finger is also low-set, so even though she knows what she wants, Shelley may find it difficult to express her opinions—particularly in romantic relationships. However, a strong Mercury line balances this, so in the business field Shelley's communication skills reign supreme. Shelley's fate line is much straighter and clearer than Avril's, indicating that she set herself on her career path at an early age. Combined with her strong Sun line, this indicates that Shelley will attain a great deal of success in her chosen field.

WHEN READING FOR A CHILD

Reading for a child is quite different from reading for an adult, because a lot of information is yet to be etched into their palms. Keep this in mind when reading, and remind the parents that what you are reading is the child's potential and that a clearer picture may not emerge until the child is in her teens or twenties.

The first thing to assess when reading for a child is the dominant feature on the hand. Is it a finger, the thumb, or one of the lines? Perhaps one of the mounts stands out. This is the way in which you'll be able to assess the child's main area of interest and where any potential talents may lie. Be wary of the so-called stage parents—people who didn't fulfill their own expectations, and so place all their faith into their child's ability to succeed. In these cases, emphasizing the importance of play and relaxation in helping to stimulate their child's creativity may help the child to avoid burnout at an early age.

Children may shy away from showing you their palms. Make the reading fun, show them your hand, and ask, "Do you have a line like this one?" If you can't coax them out of their shell, postpone the reading—only read for an interested and enthusiastic subject.

ROSIE, 3, RIGHT-HANDED

POINTS OF INTEREST
- Long, strong lines
- Fate line
- Long, straight head line
- Dominant Mercury finger

NOTES

The hands of children are always intriguing because all their potential can be seen. So much of Rosie's character is already etched into her palm at a very young age. Her life line is long and deeply etched, and curves around the palm to end near the wrist. This indicates a smooth passage through life, with only minor health problems.

Rosie has a very long head line, which travels almost all the way across her palm. It is quite straight, showing a logical mind and a sharp intellect. Her heart line is very curved and ends near the Jupiter finger. This indicates a wildly romantic nature, and that she will be quick to fall in love but happy to shrug her shoulders and move on.

As we would expect with the hands of a child, both palms are fairly similar. Rosie has not yet had the opportunity to make her own path in life. However, her palms have already begun to alter, as her parents have noticed since they have been taking Rosie's handprints each year since she was born. Rosie already has the start of a fate line, which many children (and some adults) do not. Hers is still quite short, but will lengthen and strengthen as she matures.

Rosie holds her Mercury finger apart from the other fingers, already displaying an independent streak. She also has a strong Mercury line, indicating a good communicator. Her fingers are long and thin, revealing artistic tendencies and a love of beauty.

Rosie's thumb is interesting, as it is low-set and held at a wide angle. This girl is bound for adventure, and nobody will be able to stand in her way.

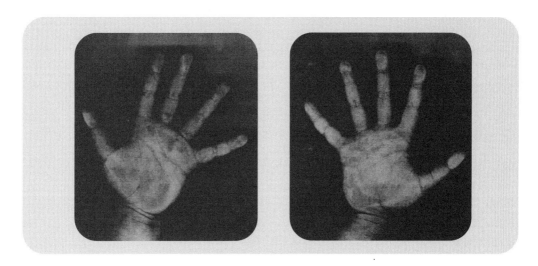

FURTHER READING

You will find numerous books on palmistry in your local bookstore or library. Here are some useful titles.

Altman, N., *The Palmistry Workbook*, The Aquarian Press, London, 1984.

Benham, W. G., *The Laws of Scientific Hand Reading*, Rider, U.K., 1946; republished as *The Benham Book of Palmistry*, Newcastle Publishing, CA, 1998.

Benham, W. G., *How to Choose Vocations from the Hand*, Newcastle Publishing, CA, 1995.

Cheiro, *Palmistry: The Language of the Hand*, Random House, New York, 1999 (1894).

Fenton, S. & Wright, M., *Palmistry*, Carlton, London, 2000.

Hutchinson, B., *Your Life in Your Hands*, Faber & Faber, London, 1933.

Reid, L., *Elements of Handreading*, Element Books Ltd., U.K., 1994.

Verner-Bonds, L., *Thorsons Way of Palmistry*, Thorsons, London, 1997.

Webster, R., *Palm Reading for Beginners*, Llewellyn Publications, St. Paul, 2000.

West, P., *The Complete Guide to Palmistry*, Element Books Ltd., London, 1998.

Whitaker, H., *Palmistry: Your Highway to Life*, Lansdowne Publishing, Sydney, 1997.

Wilson, J., *The Complete Book of Palmistry*, Bantam Books, New York, 1971.

GLOSSARY

You will find that the terminology of palmistry varies in different books on the subject and also depends on the palmist's influences and training. Here are some common terms used in palmistry, along with their variations.

Active hand: The hand a person uses most, e.g., for writing; the dominant hand. Reveals what a person has made of their life.

Air hand: Some hand readers classify hands by the elements (Air, Earth, Fire, Water). This classification comes from the Middle Ages, when people had a fascination with astrology rather than with the traditional hand shapes. This elemental hand type has a square palm and long fingers.

Allergy line: A line that runs parallel to the wrist across the base of Luna; also called the **poison line** or **line of escape**. People with this marking need to be cautious, as they are likely to suffer from allergies or react negatively to various substances (e.g., by becoming dependent on alcohol or drugs).

Apollo finger: The third (ring) finger, which reveals a person's creativity and potential for success.

Bar: A short line that usually crosses through a line, indicating that there was an obstruction (physical or abstract) in this area.

Battle cross: A cross that appears in the center of the palm, normally between the life and fate lines. In ancient times, this formation meant a noble death in battle, but it now means a person who is intensely dedicated to a cause.

Bracelets: Lines that form semicircular markings just under the palm around the wrist; also known as **rascettes**.

Chain: A formation comprising a small group of islands, which join together to form a chain. This indicates a period of turmoil or upheaval.

Children lines: Fine vertical lines that rise from the marriage lines on the outer edge of the palm. These lines indicate a person's potential for having (or caring for) children.

Conic hand: One of the classifications for hand shape. A conic hand has fingers with rounded tips and the palm more rectangular than square.

Creative curve: The name for the curve on the outer edge of the palm (near the mount of Luna).

Cross: A marking that may appear on any part of the palm. See **battle cross, mystic cross**.

Droplets: Small, rounded formations, resembling drops of water, that appear on the center of the upper phalange of the fingers.

Earth hand: Elemental hand shape with a square palm and short fingers.

Empty hand: A hand with very few visible lines apart from the primary lines.

Family ring: A (usually) chained line that runs around the base of the thumb.

Fate line: The line that runs from the base of the palm to the Saturn (middle) finger, sometimes called the career line.

Fire hand: This elemental hand shape has a rectangular palm and shortish fingers.

Girdle of Venus: Two or three short, broken, or chained lines that run horizontally under the Jupiter (index), Saturn (middle), or Apollo (ring) fingers.

Great quadrangle: The area between the head line and the heart line.

Grille: Any formation of small horizontal or vertical lines that are close together in a grille shape, indicating a period of frustration or disorientation.

Half-moons: The white semicircular shapes found at the base of some fingernails.

Head line: One of the four major lines. It runs across the palm, usually starting midway between the thumb and the Jupiter (index) finger, below the heart line. When the head line crosses the palm completely from one side to the other, it is known as the **Sydney line**.

Health line: A line that is also known as the **Mercury line**, often confused with the Apollo line, but easily identifiable because of its placement under the Mercury (little) finger.

Health mount: The bulge that appears on the edge of the hand, between the thumb and the Jupiter (index) finger when a tight fist is formed. If this mount is firm and full, good health is indicated.

Heart line: The upper line on the palm, starting under the Mercury (little) finger and running across the palm.

Hollow palm: A palm with an apparent indentation in the center. Traditionally, this meant that the person would never be short of money. However, it can also mean a person who is overly cautious.

Islands: Oval markings that appear within the lines on the palm and indicate a period of upheaval.

Jupiter finger: The index finger, which reveals a person's spirituality and success.

Knots: Bulges at the joints of the fingers. These are relevant to palmistry only if they occur naturally, not through arthritis or injury.

Life line: The line that runs around the base of the thumb (the mount of Venus).

Line of escape: A line that runs straight across the base of the palm from the mount of Venus to the mount of Luna. Also known as the **allergy line** or **poison line**.

Line of intuition: A curve that runs from the mount of Luna to the mount of Mercury. When present on the palm, it indicates a person of high sensitivity.

Lines of influence: These lines rise from any of the primary lines and indicate a positive outcome to a difficult situation.

Lucky M: On some hands the heart line, head line, fate line, and life line are arranged in such a manner that the letter M is formed. This is a fortunate formation, indicating luck with marriage and money.

Major lines: The four primary lines visible on most hands—the life line, the head line, the heart line, and the fate line.

Marriage lines: Small horizontal line or lines between the Mercury (little) finger and the heart line, revealing the number of serious relationships a person may experience in his or her life.

Mars inner (positive) mount: The fleshy mount found between the mounts of Venus and Jupiter.

Mars outer (negative) mount: The fleshy mount found between the mounts of Luna and Mars.

Medical stigmata: Three or more short, vertical lines found on the mount of Mercury, indicating the capacity to heal.

Mercury finger: The little finger, which governs communication and success in business.

Mercury line: This line, also known as the **health line**, is sometimes called the liver line, as it was believed that the line indicated the state of the liver.

Mixed hand: One of the classifications for hand shape. Contains two or more features of other hand types.

Money lines: Rare formations on the palm that can indicate a person will come into money in an unusual manner, such as through inheritance or a lottery.

Mount of Apollo: The fleshy area under the Apollo (ring) finger.

Mount of Jupiter: The fleshy pad under the Jupiter (index) finger.

Mount of Luna: The fleshy mount on the lower percussion side of the hand.

Mount of Mercury: The fleshy mound lying at the base of the Mercury (little) finger.

Mount of Saturn: The fleshy mound under the Saturn (middle) finger.

Mount of Venus: The large mount at the base of the thumb, considered the third phalange of the thumb.

Mystic cross: An X that may appear between the heart line and the head line. Its presence indicates an interest in the occult.

Passive hand: The hand a person uses least; reveals a person's destiny.

Percussion: The outer (instinctive) side of the hand.

Phalange: The sections of the fingers and the thumbs. Fingers have three phalanges. The thumb has two, with the mount of Venus considered the third.

Plain of Mars: The section between the positive and negative mounts of Mars.

Poison line: A line running straight across the mount of Luna to the life line, a warning that the person could have problems with excessive use of substances or could experience major allergies. Also known as the **allergy line** or **line of escape**.

Psychic hand: One of the classifications for hand shape. Psychic hands have long and slender palms and fingers, with pointed fingertips.

Radial side: The active, or thumb, side of the hand.

Rascettes: The traditional term for the bracelet markings around the wrist.

Ring of Solomon: More a line than a traditional ring shape, found under the Apollo (ring) finger.

Saturn finger: The second (middle) finger, which relates to seriousness and responsibility.

Simian line: A line found on some palms where the head and the heart lines appear as one line.

Spatulate hand: One of the classifications for hand shape. These hands usually have fingers that splay out at the tips or palms that are narrow at one end and broad at the other.

Square: A formation that may appear on the palms or the fingers.

Square hand: One of the classifications for hand shape. These hands have square palms with no rounded features and the fingertips appear flat on top.

Star: A series of lines forming a star shape, which may appear anywhere on the palms or fingers.

Sun line: Sometimes called the Apollo line, this is a line that runs up the palm to end under the Apollo (ring) finger.

Sydney line: The name for the head line when this line crosses the palm completely from one side to the other.

Teacher's square: A number of lines forming a square on the mount of Jupiter, indicating a person with a talent for teaching.

Travel lines: A series of lines that run inward from the percussion side of the palm onto the palm, usually appearing on the mount of Luna but sometimes extending up to the mount of Mercury.

Triangle: A fortunate marking that

strengthens the meaning of any feature it appears on.

Trident: A line ending in a triple formation; a sign of fortune, as it indicates perfect balance.

Water hand: This elemental hand shape consists of a rectangular palm and long fingers.

Worry lines: A lot of fine lines on the surface of the palm, showing nervous tension. The more lines on a person's hand, the more on that person's mind. Vertical lines on the base phalanges of the fingers can also indicate worries.

Writer's fork: The presence of a two-pronged fork at the end of the head line, indicating that the subject has a talent for writing. This is particularly so if the fork ends on the mount of Luna, indicating creativity.

INDEX

QUICK REFERENCE GUIDE

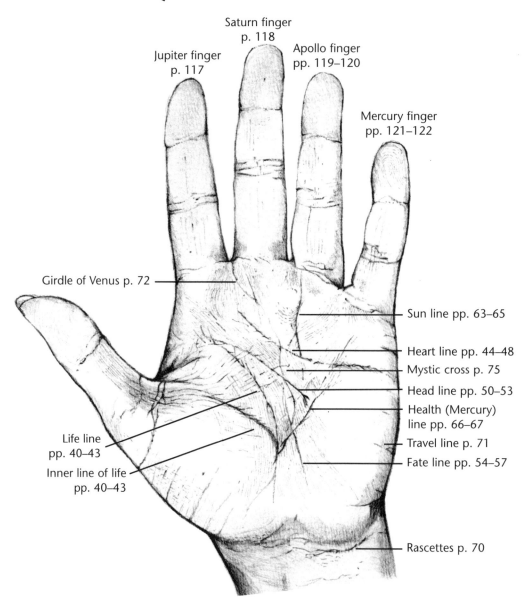

Saturn finger
p. 118

Jupiter finger
p. 117

Apollo finger
pp. 119–120

Mercury finger
pp. 121–122

Girdle of Venus p. 72

Sun line pp. 63–65

Heart line pp. 44–48

Mystic cross p. 75

Head line pp. 50–53

Health (Mercury)
line pp. 66–67

Travel line p. 71

Fate line pp. 54–57

Life line
pp. 40–43

Inner line of life
pp. 40–43

Rascettes p. 70

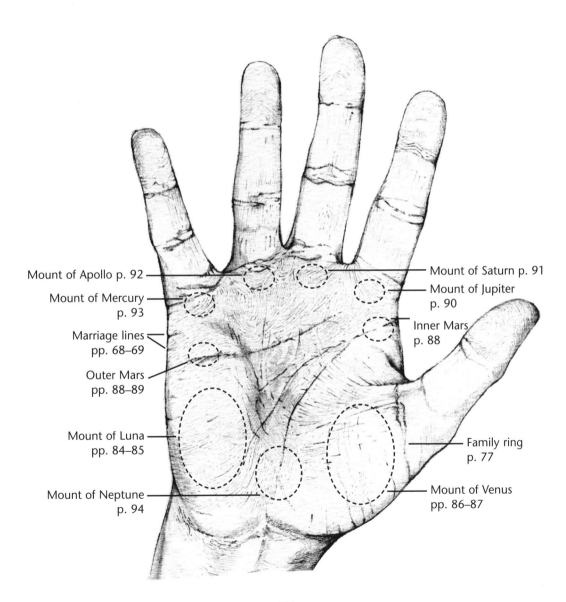

Mount of Apollo p. 92

Mount of Mercury
p. 93

Marriage lines
pp. 68–69

Outer Mars
pp. 88–89

Mount of Luna
pp. 84–85

Mount of Neptune
p. 94

Mount of Saturn p. 91

Mount of Jupiter
p. 90

Inner Mars
p. 88

Family ring
p. 77

Mount of Venus
pp. 86–87

SPECIAL MARKINGS

 Islands are a disturbance in the line, a time of difficulty that can be overcome.

 Chains are periods of turmoil, emotional or physical, usually occurring in childhood or adolescence.

 Grilles usually indicate a problem that can be readily solved.

 Forks show the two different directions a person can take, and usually mean a positive balance.

 A **square**, when it appears over a break in a line, means protection wherever it occurs.

 Breaks in lines indicate a major change.

 When **a line breaks and starts again elsewhere**, this indicates a change of direction.

 A **cross** has significance; its meaning depends on where it occurs, but it's a positive sign.

 Stars indicate good fortune; where that fortune arises depends on where the star is located.

 Triangles are fortunate, particularly when they occur on a line.

 Circles are very rare, but they usually indicate a period where freedom is restricted.

 Bars across a line indicate barriers, so the subject has to be inventive to overcome them.

 Doubled lines are most fortunate because the line now has double strength.

 **Tridents** are the most fortunate of line endings because they are the perfect balance of all its properties.

 When a line's **ending is frayed**, then energy tends to be fragmented and weakened at the end of life.

 Dots can appear on lines and usually indicate a problem that has arisen at this particular time.